i

FLY FISHING THE PACIFIC NORTHWEST:
A Beginner's Guide

By Daniel Green

ISBN 9781790486090
Cover photographs by Gary Bevers, Woodland, Washington.

Contents

Preface

The purpose of this book is to help beginners learn the basics of fly fishing, with an emphasis on fly fishing in the Pacific Northwest. Why in the Pacific Northwest? For me the decision was easy. It is the only place I have ever fly-fished and I have fished here for nearly forty years. But I'd be a fool to complain. It is a beautiful area, full of excellent fly fishing opportunities.

Is the Pacific Northwest so different from other regions that it requires a separate book? It doesn't **require** such a book, but the beginner will benefit from information specific to our region. Much of our fly fishing techniques and writings came from the East Coast and England. Conditions are different in those places, and some of the skills and priorities need to be adjusted for fishing the Pacific Northwest.

Part I is a quick overview of the Pacific Northwest from an angling perspective. The reader will want to supplement this information with more detailed books and articles which have been written for specific rivers and lakes in the area.

Part II covers the basic skills: proper gear, casting, fly choice, basic trout biology, basic insect study, presenting the fly, playing fish, etc.

Part III goes beyond the technical skills and addresses the "softer" but no less important skills such as ethics, environmental issues, literature, and traditions. Many modern introductory books contain nothing on these topics. This is a huge mistake. With increasing numbers of anglers and other users competing for the same resources, etiquette is more important than ever. Environmental concerns have grown over the decades and the sins of earlier generations have come home to roost. One can fly fish successfully and enjoy the sport without appreciating its historical roots and rich literary traditions, but much enjoyment is missed.

I have laid out the basic skills, but have also shared personal stories, gleaned from my forty-some years of fly fishing, which I hope will reinforce the material and provide a personal touch. These personal musings have been set in a narrower margin and in italic. So, if you want to skip an old man's reminiscences you can do so easily. But I hope you will take a peek. Could be something worthwhile.

What's changed in forty years? A lot more people chasing fewer fish. Increased harvest and shrinking habitat have taken their toll. Anglers now need to travel further to find decent fishing.

But there are some signs of progress. I have discussed these in Chapter 5. Perhaps we are on the cusp of a new, improved era of sport fishing in the Pacific Northwest. Perhaps that's over-optimistic.

I would like to thank the many folks that have helped me with this volume. Gabe Green for his excellent photographs of fly patterns found in Chapter 12. Gary Bevers for his beautiful Atlantic salmon flies that he both tied and photographed that grace the cover and Chapter 12, as well as for his advice and encouragement. My dad, Bill Green, for teaching me to cast and tie flies, as well as untold other lessons for 60 years. John Geyer for his stunning photographs found in several chapters. For the many friends who reviewed drafts and gave valuable input.

I would like to thank the Fly Fishers International for their permission to include quotes from their *Code of Angling Ethics* in Chapter 18, and for its inclusion as Appendix 2.

And a special thanks to my editors: Nate Green of Idaho, my ever-patient wife Teresa, and our good friend Deborah White. They chased down typos and errors and offered valuable advice that, in the end, made this a better book.

And a special thanks to all those unknown anglers I have met streamside who have taught me much.

Part 1: The Pacific Northwest

1. An Angler's Paradise

The Pacific Northwest is an angler's paradise. It is a diverse region of beautiful rivers, lakes, Puget Sound, and several major mountain ranges. There are no exact boundaries of the Pacific Northwest; the boundaries in this chapter are formed in large part by my own experience. You will over time create your own mental map of the region.

The mighty Columbia River cuts through the heart of the region. Twelve hundred miles long, it is the largest river on the West Coast. Prior to the coming of Europeans to the Pacific Northwest, the river hosted the largest population of salmon and steelhead in the world, totaling as many as 16 million returning adult fish, all wild. Today at most 1 million adults, mostly of hatchery origin, return each year. Hydroelectric power dams, overfishing, and strip-mine-style logging have each taken their toll. Progress, you know.

Keep in mind that this book is not a guide book on where to fish the Pacific Northwest. Excellent guidebooks are available that will provide you with detailed information on the specific rivers and lakes you want to fish, what gear and flies to use, the best seasons to fish, where to stay, etc. This chapter will give you a strategic overview to help you get started.

EAST–WEST DIVIDE

Look at the map on the next page. The Cascade Mountains form a 700-mile-long divide between east and west. The fishing is quite different on each side. Understanding this east/west divide from an angling perspective is an essential starting point.

WEST SIDE: Rain Forests and Nurseries for Anadromous Fish

The climate on the west slope of the Cascade Range is a temperate mix of mild winters and plentiful rainfall. The soil here tends toward acidic, which causes rivers and lakes to yield relatively sparse insect life and therefore tend not to be prolific producers of resident trout. The rivers on the west side are primarily nurseries for sea-going salmonids: steelhead, sea-run cutthroat trout, and five of the six species of Pacific salmon. These fish begin life as eggs in the gravel of their natal streams, then become tiny one-inch babies who live and grow for two or three years in the stream, then migrate to the ocean and feed for one to five years, growing prodigious on the ocean's bounty, then return to their natal rivers to spawn.

Anglers from other regions often travel here during the summer with their fly gear and skills honed back home, fish the rivers, and leave disappointed. There is nothing wrong with their techniques nor their flies. There just are not many resident trout in our rivers. After hours of fruitless casting, they may catch a few seven-inch, silver-colored "trout." These are *smolts*, baby salmon or steelhead migrating out to the ocean. *They are not legitimate quarry for the angler*; they need to be released unharmed to continue to the ocean and return as huge steelhead and salmon. Adjusting to this reality is a first step in understanding fishing in the soggy west side.

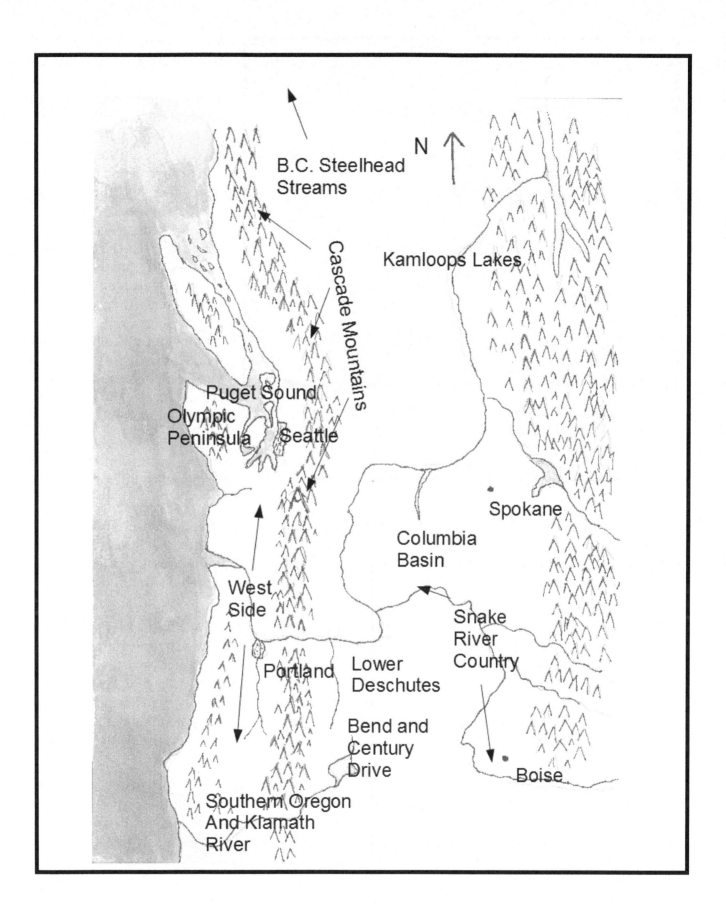

B.C. Steelhead
Streams

N ↑

Kamloops Lakes

Cascade Mountains

Puget Sound
Olympic
Peninsula   Seattle

Spokane

Columbia
Basin

West
Side

Snake
River
Country

Portland

Lower
Deschutes

Bend and
Century
Drive

Boise

Southern Oregon
And Klamath
River

Dale Fredrickson prepares to release a magnificent Wind River steelhead. Photo by John Geyer.

An exception to this general rule exists in those stream headwaters to which anadromous fish cannot ascend due to high waterfalls or dams lacking fish passage. In the headwaters above these obstructions, resident trout live out their entire lives. The fish, like the streams they live in, are small. But it can be lots of fun. First, study maps, talk to people, and identify these headwaters. Then explore. A four-weight rod with a floating line and a box of Elk-hair Caddis dry flies are all you need. That, and a pair of sturdy legs and an adventuresome spirit.

The lakes are another matter. There are many lakes in the area that can provide excellent fly fishing for trout. Aided by mild winters, anglers here can extend the fly fishing season over several more months than can residents of Michigan or Montana.

Salmon and steelhead are kings out here. Steelhead, as explained in Chapter 5, are rainbow trout that migrate to the ocean and return to their natal river to spawn. Anglers seasonally anticipate runs of these beautiful fish on local streams. For the angler, understanding the timing of these runs is critical. A period of days may change a river from being barren of catchable fish to hosting good numbers of eight-pound winter steelhead.

What about fly fishing for Pacific salmon and steelhead? Both are possible. Pacific salmon present some challenges and limitations for the fly fisher. They do not take a fly well after they return to fresh water. See my discussion in Chapter 10. Steelhead are the premier Pacific Northwest fish to take on a fly, but for the beginner it can be like trying to learn to drive in the Indy 500. I recommend the beginning fly angler seek out opportunities to catch resident trout on a fly, then having mastered the basics, expand his or her skills to include fly fishing for steelhead and Pacific salmon. Steelhead have been called the "fish of a thousand casts." They are difficult to take on the fly or any other method.

West side lakes and rivers produce fewer insects than on the east side. There are insect hatches on the west side, though, and flies can be tied to imitate them and catch trout. It's just that you won't experience the huge hatches of insects that other parts of the country do. The sport of fly fishing in the United States developed along streams in the Catskill Mountains in New York State, the LeTort in Pennsylvania, and other northeastern streams. Along these hallowed waters the sport grew, and prolific mayfly hatches led to expertise in "matching the hatch": Anglers studied the emergences of the local hatches and tied exact imitations to match them. Literally thousands of unique patterns were developed. In the Pacific Northwest we do have hatches, you can identify patterns to imitate them; it is just a matter of a change in emphasis. There just are not as many hatches. You need to learn to fish when there doesn't appear to be a hatch and the fish are feeding opportunistically.

EAST SIDE: Sunshine and Leaping Rainbows

The east side sits in a rain shadow formed by the Cascade Mountains. Compared to the west side, the soil is very alkaline, resulting in greater weed growth and therefore more insect life and more and bigger trout. These are generalizations and the reader can find exceptions. Here the winters are cold. During long, summer days, the sun beats down unmercifully, ripening grapes that in the fall will be crushed and bottled into rich, red wines that rival Napa Valley's offerings. Here the wind, unfettered by forest or hill, blows unmercifully across a stark landscape formed by ancient volcanic activity and ice-age floods. The east side landscape is an acquired taste.

The richness of the water here allows many east side streams to support both resident and migratory rainbow (steelhead) trout races. Examples include the Deschutes, Klickitat, and Methow rivers. The steelhead runs here are almost always summer-run, as opposed to the predominant winter-runs of the west side.

The east side is well-known to anglers for its lake fishing. The alkaline water yields rich harvests of chironomids, mayflies and damselflies. If you could pick a lake and observe it every few days from March through July, you would witness a slow parade of insects, each hatching during its appointed time. Many of these lakes are well-known and you won't be fishing alone.

The area's rainbows are primarily a subspecies known as "redband" rainbows. The redband rainbows can be differentiated from the "coastal" rainbows by their more vivid red stripe down their lateral lines.

Also present are cutthroat trout. The cutthroats here belong to different subspecies than found on the west side. On the west side, the cutthroats are almost always the *coastal cutthroat* subspecies; on the east side are found two other subspecies: the *Lahontan cutthroat*, an import from Nevada; and the *westslope cutthroat*, a trout native to this area. (The westslope cutthroat name refers to the westslope of the Continental Divide, not to the westslope of the Cascade Range.)

The Lahontan cutthroat evolved in the highly alkaline waters of the ancient Lake Lahontan in what is today Nevada. Lake Lenore, near the town of Soap Lake, Washington, held no trout of any kind due to its extremely high alkalinity until fisheries biologists brought in Lahontan cutthroat from Nevada. They have thrived in Lenore, and now have also been planted in nearby Grimes and Omak lakes.

Brown trout are present here also. They are all imports, being native only to Europe. They thrive here in many of the lakes and in a few rivers.

2. West of the Divide

Here are four destinations west of the divide I'd like to highlight:

British Columbia Steelhead Streams

Six hundred miles north of Seattle, sandwiched between rugged mountain ranges, the Skeena River and its celebrated tributaries the Kispiox, Babine, and Bulkley, plunge to the ocean. These and other nearby streams host some of the finest runs of steelhead in the world.

A bucket list item for me.

The specialized techniques for catching steelhead on a fly are outside the scope of this book, but the basic skills described in the following chapters will form a solid foundation upon which you can build the advanced skills needed to catch these magnificent steelhead trout.

The Olympic Peninsula

The Olympic Peninsula is a remote, temperate rainforest wedged between Puget Sound and the Pacific Ocean. The Olympic National Park sits at the heart of the region and ensures that at least the headwaters of its rivers are protected from the overzealous logging that has damaged watersheds throughout the Pacific Northwest. Besides being an area providing excellent fly fishing, the Olympic Peninsula is also a prime destination for camping, hiking, and vacationing all summer long.

Winter-run steelhead and sea-run cutthroats are kings here. There are also some trout opportunities in the lakes. Forks, Washington, a small town on the west side of the peninsula, has one of the highest annual rainfall levels of any settlement in the contiguous United States: 119.7 inches per year. Bring your raincoat.

Puget Sound

Puget Sound is a 12,000-square-mile, salt-water bay. During the last ice-age, advancing and retreating glaciers carved out its numerous octopus-like tentacles. Seattle, Tacoma, Olympia, and Bellevue lay on the eastern shore, and are home to some 3.8 million persons. Not a pristine wilderness, but the scenery is stunning, and often you cannot see any evidence that you are near a major population center.

The tides come and go twice a day here. Being aware of the tides is essential to not just your angling success but also to your safety. An area that was covered by water when you arrived at 10 AM could be, at 1 PM, a quarter-mile-wide mudflat.

The primary targets for the fly angler in Puget Sound are "resident" salmon and sea-run cutthroat. Both fish utilize Puget Sound as their "ocean": they spawn in the streams, the babies spend a few years in that natal stream growing, then migrate to Puget Sound and gain most of their growth in that marine environment. The cutthroats grow to a hefty 12 to 18 inches, then return in the fall and winter to spawn. The resident salmon, primarily silver and king salmon, follow a similar life history strategy, though all Pacific salmon die directly after spawning. Unlike the huge silvers and king salmon that migrate to the ocean proper, these fish are smaller, reaching perhaps 16 to 20 inches in length just prior to their spawning run.

Surprisingly, fly fishing in Puget Sound does **not** require a boat. The shorelines are easy to wade and the fish tend to hug the shoreline. However, a boat will allow you to hop from beach to beach in search of fish and legitimately thumb your nose at "no trespassing" signs.

West Side of the Cascades and the Pacific Coast

This vast region contains excellent steelhead and salmon streams but also some wonderful fly fishing lakes. The streams generally follow the pattern of nurseries for anadromous trout and salmon as described above. The Stillaguamish is described in Chapter 19. The Skagit is a huge river famous for its winter-run steelhead. The Kalama, Washougal, Wind, and Lewis rivers in Southwest Washington produce summer and winter-run steelhead as well as salmon. Further south in Oregon, the Santiam and Clackamas rivers provide the same.

Several lakes have been set aside for fly fishing only or are managed under restrictive regulations. Pass Lake north of Seattle, and Merrill and Coldwater lakes near Mount St. Helens are a few that I have enjoyed for decades. Don't overlook the colder months of the year: Our winters here are mild, regulations often allow year-round angling, and thus some excellent fishing can be had when others are zonking out on TV re-runs.

Sea-run cutthroats are a favorite of fly fishers. They are beautiful, fight well, and hit a fly aggressively. This region is smack-dab in the middle of their range. Unfortunately, they are very sensitive to environmental degradation and their numbers throughout this region are much reduced from historical levels. The Cowlitz River, a major tributary of the Columbia, hosts a large hatchery run of these fish that return each September and October.

Al Wood works a fly across the plunge pool at the base of breathtaking Lower Falls on the Lewis River. Photo by John Geyer.

The Coastal Mountain Range divides this region through Southwest Washington and most of Oregon. On the west slope of this range, a multitude of relatively short streams carry the area's prodigious winter rainfall from the hillsides to the Pacific Ocean. Highway 101 follows the coast and crosses these streams within sight of the ocean. Here, the star performers are the coho (silver) salmon, the sea-run cutthroat trout, and the winter-run steelhead.

9

3. East Side Destinations

Among the many east side possibilities, here are a few to look at a little closer:

Kamloops Region

An eight-hour drive north from Seattle will take the reader into British Columbia and to a dry, sparsely populated region of rolling hills, ponderosa pine stands, and hundreds of lakes. The star performer here is a strain of redband rainbow called the Kamloops trout. All rainbows have a reputation for jumping but the Kamloops trout is the leaper par excellence. Boy, do they jump! And run, and fight. These trout thrive in the lakes of this region and are what has made this area famous among anglers.

If you travel to the Kamloops region it is essential that you research beforehand and identify the lakes that should be productive during your visit. Generally, the spring is productive, summer is too hot, then fall has potential also. Winter–forget it. Also, the higher the elevation of the lake, the later in the spring the lake will become productive.

Columbia Basin

With its forbidding-looking terrain, hot summers and ice-cold winters, this area may not be the ideal place for a family vacation, but the fly fishing opportunities, especially for trout, are legendary.

The terrain, in large part, was formed by the Missoula floods 15,000 years ago. One result of these floods was Crab Creek, a 164-mile-long, slow-moving creek that meanders through the region. Prior to the 1950s, for most of its length, the creek flowed too slow and warm to host any fish but carp and other rough fish. Then in the 1950s, irrigation activity in the nearby farms raised the water table several feet and caused new cold-water lakes to literally pop up out of the desert along Crab Creek. The state game department saw the opportunity and launched a stocking program managed for trophy trout utilizing Kamloops-strain rainbows. Lenice, Nunnally, and Merry are some of those lakes. Also in this watershed runs Rocky Ford Creek, a true "spring creek." In angling parlance, a spring creek is a slow-moving, cold-water stream with prolific insect life and often large, wary trout. Its source is underground springs rather than the typical mountain headwaters of most streams. There are a few of these in the Pacific Northwest: Rocky Ford Creek in Washington and Silver Creek in Idaho are the two I am familiar with.

The Yakima River flows about 200 miles from the east slope of the Cascade Mountains to join the Columbia River near Tri-Cities, Washington. It hosts wild rainbow trout and fly fishing can be excellent. However, there are numerous irrigation dams throughout its length, and they affect the river flows, which in turn affect the fishing. Generally, the river flows high all summer to aid irrigation, then it drops and clears during the fall and winter. But good fishing can be had even during the high flows of summer, though you will need a boat and solid boating skills. Be sure to get up-to-date information on flow levels and conditions before you go.

The Columbia Basin presents challenges to go with the opportunities. The desert winds blow strong across the flat landscape, and you must have proper shelter. I have seen tents literally torn to shreds. The nights can be ice-cold here even in late spring. Many of these lakes become too warm during the summer for good fishing.

Bend and Century Drive

Bend, Oregon, sits near the east slope of the Cascades at about 3,500 feet elevation. The scenery is stunning. The area is a Mecca for outdoor recreation: skiing, mountain biking, climbing, rafting, and fly fishing. Unlike the Columbia Basin, the area is ideal for family vacations, and visiting anglers will have company. Campgrounds here fill up quick, so make reservations early.

The Upper Deschutes River flows through Bend and provides excellent rainbow and brown trout fly fishing. Fall River is a spring creek that hosts good populations of rainbow, brook and brown trout. The water runs clear and cold.

A solitary angler works through a nice drift on Central Oregon's Crooked River. Photo by John Geyer.

This region is probably best known for its highly productive and beautiful lakes. There are dozens that are excellent for fly fishing, but I'll mention just a few: Crane Prairie, Hosmer, Lava, Sparks, East, and Cultus lakes. Be sure to note the altitude of the lakes you plan to fish and this will help you determine when the snow has cleared and the lake can be accessed. There are fly shops in the area that can help you sort out the flies and techniques to get you started.

Lower Deschutes River

Perched to the east of the Cascade Mountains, the Deschutes flows northward over 250 miles from its headwaters near Little Lava Lake to its confluence with the Columbia River. It is one of the finest fly fishing streams in North America. The Upper and Lower Deschutes are divided by the Pelton Dam about one hundred miles upstream from the mouth.

The Lower Deschutes River hosts both steelhead and resident rainbow trout, nicknamed "redsides." These trout can be found throughout the length of the river. Adult redsides average a plump 12-16 inches. When hooked, they fight hard and use the strong currents to advantage. There are days when they rise boldly to flies with seeming abandon. Then there are days when they seem to be missing in action, rejecting every skillfully-tied fly in our boxes. That's fishing.

The summer steelhead begin arriving at the river mouth by late July, then can be found all the way up to the Pelton Dam by fall. Summer-runs include both wild and hatchery fish, and also fish that will stay and spawn in the Deschutes River and "upstream" fish that will continue on to spawn in upstream tributaries such as the Clearwater River in Idaho. To avoid the Columbia's warm summer water, these Clearwater fish enter the Deschutes in late summer, and remain there until cooling waters in the fall spur them to rejoin the Columbia and swim on upstream to the Snake River, then finally, months after leaving the ocean, to the Clearwater.

For the beginner, the river can be daunting. So get some help. Talk to the local fly shops, go with experienced anglers, or hire a guide. It helps to have at least several days in a row on the water; this I've found to be true with most lakes and rivers in this chapter. It may take the first day to just figure out what is going on and where you can access the water. A quick stop for an hour's fly fishing while you are out traveling can be fun but don't count on it being productive.

Also in this area is some great fly fishing for bass. Scout out the areas along the Columbia River near the mouth of the Deschutes then downstream past the town of The Dalles. You will find numerous ponds caused by the rising of the water table due to the Columbia River dams. In these warm-water ponds, small-mouth bass can provide excellent fly fishing.

Snake River Country

The northern stretch of the Snake River forms the boundary between Washington and Idaho, and then to the south between Oregon and Idaho. Thousands of steelhead swim through the Snake and return to the Dworshak National Fish Hatchery on the Clearwater River, a tributary of the Snake. The Snake itself is fly fished by anglers who cast the large, two-handed spey rods needed to reach across this wide river.

Flowing eastward out of the Blue Mountains, the Grande Ronde joins the Snake near the Washington-Oregon border. It is a premiere steelhead stream, prized by generations of fly anglers. Its broad, gentle drifts lend themselves to drifting a fly, and its 3-to-5-pound steelhead respond well to surface or near-surface fly presentations.

East of Boise, Idaho, the South Fork Boise River yields excellent resident-trout fly fishing to both bank and drift-boat anglers. Further east, the Sun Valley area offers rainbow and cutthroat fly fishing along the Big Wood River. This small stream is excellent for beginners and experienced alike: It is easy to wade, access is plentiful, and trout can be taken by a variety of techniques. I have relatives in this area and have enjoyed fishing this stream for decades. South a few miles, where Ernest Hemingway fished and hunted ducks, is world-famous Silver Creek. It is a classic spring creek, filled with large, difficult trout. I have fished this stream three times and have yet to catch a fish.

4. Southern Oregon and the Klamath River

The east–west divide I harped on earlier seems to break down somewhere in Oregon, and the streams in Southern Oregon and Northern California often host resident trout as well as salmon and steelhead. Also, the steelhead here take on a different complexion: Many streams host runs of "half-pounder" steelhead, which behave and look more like resident trout. Half-pounders don't weigh eight ounces; they typically run a plump 12 to 15 inches in length, bright-silver upon returning from the ocean, and usually weigh about a pound or so. These little silver bullets are born in the rivers, spend a year or two there, go to the ocean in the spring, stay just a few months, then return to the river in the fall of the same year. They may stay through the winter then go back to the ocean in the spring, then return in the fall, this time 18 to 20 inches long and sexually mature. They are found only in Oregon's Rogue and California's Klamath and Eel rivers.

Three large, famous rivers dominate this area: the Rogue, the Umpqua, and the Klamath. Each has a long, illustrious fly fishing history. There are excellent guide books written for each of these three rivers.

The Rogue River begins high in the Cascades and flows west 215 miles to the Pacific Ocean near the Oregon-California border. Certain sections host resident trout; the lower section hosts adult steelhead, half-pounder steelhead, and Chinook and coho salmon.

The Umpqua River includes the South and North forks. The North Fork is the most important for fly fishers. This famous river begins at nearly 6,000 feet elevation in the Cascades in the Mount Thielsen Wilderness, then flows west about one hundred miles to join the South Fork near the town of Roseburg, Oregon. Its source at nearly 6,000 feet elevation ensures that the stream flows cold all summer long thus supporting its world-famous race of summer-run steelhead.

The Klamath is unusual because it begins on the east slope of the Cascade Mountains, then carves its way through the Cascades, then continues west to carve through the Klamath Mountains, and finally joins the Pacific Ocean near Redwood National Park. Two-hundred sixty-three miles of wild trout stream, daring us to try.

The Klamath drainage begins in Oregon high-desert country near the town of Klamath Falls. Here the Williamson, the Sprague, and the Wood rivers flow into Upper Klamath Lake. This entire region has excellent fly fishing opportunities for large trout. Much of the water flows through private property, so be sure to do your homework prior to your trip.

The Upper Klamath River proper begins as the outlet of Upper Klamath Lake. The upper river hosts some excellent fly fishing for resident rainbows, but access can be tricky, so get out the maps and talk to those who know.

The Upper Klamath crosses the Oregon-California line about 25 miles east of Interstate-5. The fishing from here to the base of Iron Gate Dam, about 15 river miles south and west, is like the upper river in Oregon. Big, mean rainbows and tough access.

Below the Iron Gate Dam, it's steelhead country. Klamath steelhead include both the half-pounders like those found in the Rogue, and adult steelhead that are "small" by steelhead standards–four to six pounds–but make up for it in fight and willingness to hit a fly. From here to the ocean the river flows through a sparsely populated wilderness area. You may encounter more bears and deer than people. California isn't all suburbs and movie stars.

The Pacific Northwest is truly a diverse and beautiful region for fly fisher as well as all who enjoy the outdoors. A few themes common throughout the region: Do your research before you go; seasonal timing is critical; be sure you have enough time at one location to figure things out. My motto: Regardless of how many decades you or I have fished, when fishing a new location, we are beginners. Seek out those with local experience.

5. Trouble in Paradise

Despite the beauty of the Pacific Northwest, its fisheries are shadows of their former glories. Anglers find they need to travel further and further from home to find decent fishing. An after-work jaunt to a nearby lake or stream has become, for most of us, a thing of the past.

As stated in Chapter 1, the Columbia River salmon and steelhead runs have shrunk from as many as 16 million fish to less than 1 million. Similar reductions have been experienced throughout the region.

> *Years ago while out fishing I chanced upon a long-time resident. We chatted about the stream and our lack of catch. He told me that as a young man he and his fishing partners would sit on the bank of the river at nearby rapids and wait. They would wait until they heard the deafening roar of a large school of salmon or steelhead pushing its way upstream through the rapids. Then, and only then, they would start fishing.*
>
> *I've never heard such a sound.*

What happened? Fisheries professionals often talk about the "4 Hs":

Habitat Degradation

Shrinking and degraded habitats loom large in the decline of our fisheries. Logging, as often practiced throughout the region, results in siltation of streams, rising water temperatures, and ultimately loss of spawning habitat. Poor mining practices also result in siltation. Nearby development often feeds runoff chemicals and other toxins into streams directly or through groundwater contamination.

Hydropower

The first hydroelectric power dam built on the Columbia was the Bonneville Dam in 1933. The original plan for the dam **included no fish passage of any kind.** This was on a dam that was built directly above tide water. If built as planned it would have effectively eliminated **every fish run in the entire Columbia/Snake basin,** except those few, such as the Cowlitz and Willamette, that entered the Columbia below the dam. Luckily the commercial fishing industry caught wind of it and forced the federal government to include fish ladders in the design.

The Columbia River currently has 14 dams on its mainstem, seven on the Snake and countless other on tributaries. Dams often prevent upstream adult fish passage, but hurt fish runs in other ways: The reservoirs upstream of the dams flood the river and eliminate spawning grounds; downstream juvenile fish get lost in the reservoirs and never continue downstream; many juveniles are chewed up in the turbines, or in some cases experience nitrogen saturation–a form of the bends–due to the depths of the reservoirs.

Harvest

People love to fish. It is one of the most popular outdoor activities in the Pacific Northwest. Couple that with the region's population growth since World War II, and the math makes clear there is no way to harvest unlimited numbers of trout and salmon and expect anything except extinction.

Overharvest started at least by the 1880s when canneries were built along both shores of the lower Columbia River to exploit the huge salmon runs the river then held. Way too many fish for the local people to eat, so let's can the fish and sell them all over the country. Now the canneries are all gone. So are most of the fish.

Hatcheries

Aren't hatcheries a good thing? We get more fish to catch and eat, so what's the problem? Hatcheries can be a good thing when they are based on sound fisheries biology. I am not of the "every hatchery is evil" school of thought. But hatchery operations have too often ignored the unique genetic makeup of wild salmon and trout in each watershed. Instead, fish stocks from one river have been out-planted across the region to streams that had their own unique strains of fish, thus compromising those stocks.

Diversity is a fundamental principle of biology. We are in danger of losing unique gene pools.

Light at the end of the Tunnel?

Despite the grim picture painted above, there are a few bright spots developing.

One is the widespread acceptance of catch and release fishing and barbless hooks. I have seen some of my friends' attitudes change 180 degrees on these issues.

State fisheries people have designated certain lakes and rivers as "quality fisheries," and in those waters have required barbless hooks, limited or no kill, and no bait allowed. The results on many waters have been impressive. In Puget Sound, sea-run cutthroat trout have been protected by catch and release regulations, and their numbers have rebounded dramatically.

In Washington State, *wild steelhead gene bank rivers* have been designated in each region. These rivers receive no steelhead hatchery plants of any kind. Instead, they are being managed to strengthen their self-sustaining wild steelhead populations.

Research into genetics of steelhead has resulted in improvements to hatchery management. Anglers and fishery managers alike have come to the realization that hatcheries are not the sole answer to declining fish stocks, and at times are a significant part of the problem.

Anadromous fish passage has returned to miles of historical habitat with the removal of many small dams, such as on the Elwa River on the Olympic Peninsula, the Hemlock Dam in the Wind River drainage in Southwest Washington, and multiple dams on the Rogue River in Southern Oregon.

Poorly designed road culverts are another barrier to fish passage throughout the region. Culverts are routinely installed where logging roads cross small streams. The straight, smooth surface of the interior of a traditional culvert results in water that is too shallow and often too high of velocity for the adult fish to cross. Replacement of old culverts with fish-friendly ones that mimic the natural streambed is another effort underway throughout the Pacific Northwest. This should open many miles of streams to spawning. Many salmonid (salmon, trout, char, grayling, and whitefish) species spawn in surprisingly tiny creeks.

In summary, huge challenges exist to bringing back fish runs in the region, but steps in the right direction are being taken. I strongly encourage the reader to get involved and help make a difference. One way to get involved is to join a fly fishing club that is active in fisheries and environmental issues.

Part 2: Basic Skills

6. The Balanced Fly Outfit

To cast and fish well, the fly outfit, from fly rod through line to leader and down to the fly itself, must be balanced. "Balanced" means each component matches the size of the other components allowing them to work as a harmonious unit. The most important balancing is between the fly rod and the line. In fly casting, it is the weight of the line that loads or bends the rod and results in a good fly cast. Fly rods and lines today use a standard line weight grading system developed by the American Fishing Tackle Manufacturers Association (AFTMA). By matching the rod to the line weight, you ensure that the weight of the line on the backcast is sufficient to load the rod and result in a good cast.

Rods of varying sizes are built to meet different fishing needs. Large, heavy rods are needed to meet one or more of the following conditions: large fish, long casting, big rivers, and large or weighted flies. These heavy rigs allow greater casting distance at a cost of less delicacy of presentation. Progressively smaller and lighter rods are needed for situations that call for delicacy of fly presentation and/or smaller flies.

The chart below lists the fly outfit sizes and their uses. From this the reader should not conclude that the new fly fisher needs to go out and buy six or eight different rods. The new angler should outfit one serviceable fly rod and use it to learn to cast and fish. He or she will probably expand their arsenal of rods over time to include both lighter and heavier rods. Experienced fly fishers often own a bewildering number of fly rods, reels, and lines, but this is consistent with dedicated followers of golf, tennis, sailing, etc. For my sins, I currently own 11 rods, just counting the ones my wife knows about. To many this would seem a Spartan, wholly inadequate accumulation.

Weight	Uses	Tippet Range	Hook Range
#3 Very Light	Trout in small streams, panfish	4X – 7X	#10 - #20
#4 Light	Trout in small streams, panfish	4X – 7X	#6 - #20
#5 Medium	Good, all-around trout rod, panfish	2X – 7X	#4 - #20
#6 Medium	Good all-around fly rod, streams, lakes, light summer steelhead, bass	2X – 6X	#4 - #20
#7 Medium	Summer steelhead, larger streams, sink-tips	0X – 4X	#4 - #14
#8 Heavy	Steelhead, larger or weighted flies	0X – 4X	#2 - #12
#10 Heavy	Steelhead and Pacific salmon	0X – 2X	#2/0 - #6

Typical line weights and their uses.

In addition to matching the weight of fly line to the fly rod, the leader "tippet" (the thinnest part of the leader) should be generally matched to the size of the fly and to the fly rod, but this matching is not as exact; it is more of a range of flies and tippets that work best together. More on this later.

Your First Fly Rod, Reel and Line

So, what's the best weight outfit to start with? Based on fishing for trout throughout the Pacific Northwest, it is my opinion that a six-weight rod is the best overall starting point for a new fly fisher. If not a six-weight, then a five-weight. Such a rod will allow you a wide variety of fly fishing situations, including stream and lake fishing, casting weighted nymphs, dry flies, and streamers. Outfit the rod with the proper line, leader, tippet and flies, learn to cast and fish with it and be comfortable with it. A six-weight rod loaded with a floating line and a basic assortment of flies is a highly versatile fishing tool.

FLY LINES

The key role played by the fly line may be a foreign concept to the new fly fisher, especially if he or she has experience with spin casting or other fishing systems. **The fly line is the heart of the rod-reel-line-leader-fly- system.** It is the weight of the line that loads (bends) the rod and causes the line, leader, and fly to be cast. The fly is just along for the ride; in fact, the weight of the fly interferes with the casting, hence the difficulty in casting large or heavy fly.

> *Years ago Lee Wulf, a famous fly fishing author, arrived at a well-known Atlantic salmon stream equipped with only a fly line, leader, and fly–no fly rod. He proceeded to cast and fish using just his arm as a fulcrum, and in short order hooked, played, and landed an Atlantic salmon. This unusual stunt demonstrated the centrality of the fly line to the fly fishing process.*

A fly line must be understood as an integrated unit, not as a quantity of line. A line has three basic variables: buoyancy, shape, and weight. These cause it to cast and behave on the water as intended by the designer.

Line Buoyancy: Floating, Sinking and Sink-tip Lines

Prior to World War II, silk lines were the standard. Varying thickness of line were spliced together to create tapers. These lines had a neutral buoyancy thus would slowly sink unless periodically dressed every few hours with muscelin to repel water and aid floatation. Some inventive-minded anglers would leave the last section of line free of dressing and allowed it to sink, thus developing the first sink-tip fly line.

Modern floating fly lines are constructed of a nylon core coated with a plastic material that includes materials that float. The coating on the finished line repels water, thus eliminating the need for periodic dressing.

In the 1960s, fly line manufactures developed full-sinking lines and a wide variety of sink-tip lines in which tips ranging in length from five to 20 feet sink with the remainder of the line floating. Sink-tips and full-sinking lines are designed to sink at varying rates measured in inches per second. Most sinking lines employ high-density materials to cause the line to sink rapidly. These lines do not cast as gracefully as a floating line and are harder to pick up off the water to re-cast.

This book concentrates on developing the skills for successful freshwater fly fishing with a floating fly line. All diagrams of an angler fly fishing, unless stated otherwise, portray an angler using a floating fly line.

Shape: Fly Line Tapers

Modern fly lines are usually 80 or 90 feet in length. Each fly line is designed with a taper, or varying diameter along its length. This shape in turn influences its casting and drifting behavior.

A *double-taper* fly line tapers equally at both ends from a fatter "belly" section. The tapering length at each end is about 10 feet. The taper at the end of the line causes the line to softly roll out onto the water as the energy is gradually dissipated. Without the taper the line will tend to slap down onto the water.

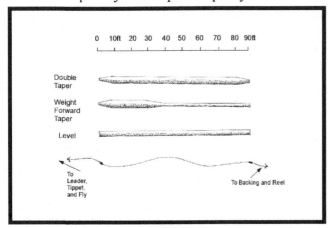

Fly line tapers.

A *weight-forward taper, or rocket taper*, is a line that has a short front taper and a long, thin section behind the belly. The weight-forward taper has advantages and disadvantages: When being cast, other than a short cast of 20-35 feet, the belly is extended completely out into the cast so that the thin section of the line is at the angler's rod tip. This allows the angler to "shoot line" during the forward cast thus allowing longer casts. On the downside, many anglers feel that weight-forward lines are more difficult to manipulate on the water and allow less delicacy of presentation.

A *level line,* as the name implies, has no forward or rear taper and therefore tends to slap down onto the water. I'm not sure why these lines are marketed. I purchased one many years ago, but found little use for it until I cut it into six foot lengths and used it to lash camping and fishing equipment together.

In addition to the above-described tapers, a bewildering armada of specialty tapers is marketed for saltwater, steelhead, bass, spey rods, and other applications.

I recommend the beginning fly fisher begin with and get comfortable with a floating fly line, either double-taper or weight-forward. Next, if the angler is going to fish lakes, I would recommend purchasing a full-sinking line for use when the fish are not feeding on or near the surface. Following the mastery of the sink line on lakes, the angler should consider sink-tips and other specialty lines. These are outside the scope of this book.

Fly Line Weights

Using the AFTMA system, typical line weights range from #3 to #10, and refer to the weight in grams of the first 30 feet of the line. Since all floating lines are made of materials of similar density, the varying weights are a result of varying diameters of line.

Lighter fly lines result in more delicate casts which help you avoid scaring fish. The heavier weight lines, all else held constant, can cast further than a light line, but at a cost of delicacy of presentation.

Line Designations

Manufactures of lines have established coding systems to assist purchasers in selecting and using their products. Putting it all together, here are some examples:

DT 6 F   Double Taper; Weight #6; Floating
WF 8 F   Weight Forward; Weight #8; Floating

This coding system pulls together the three basic dimensions of the fly line:

Shape   Weight Buoyancy

Some manufacturers include a little tag or sticker that you can use to keep track of your lines. A pet peeve of mine is that many lines have nothing on them to indicate their dimensions. When you start out and only have one line matching your one rod you have no problem. But if you are like most of us, in 10 years you will have four or five rods and 10 or 15 lines. With the importance we have placed on proper line selection, how are you going to know which is which? I have resorted to a system of tags attached to each line.

Care and Maintenance of Fly Lines

The modern fly line requires very little maintenance, but there are a few things you need to do to protect your investment. Lines should not be stored permanently on a reel. Being stored on a reel forces the line into tight coils that will eventually take a set, resulting in a permanently kinky line. Periodically you should wind the line off the reel either onto a #10 coffee can or in large loose loops of about 12-16 inches in diameter. During the off-season–for me December through February–I store my lines in the latter fashion. Prior to shelving them I also pull the line through a soft rag soaked in line conditioner. This cleans the line and treats it as well. You don't need to take the line off the reel every time you fish; just once every few months or at least at the end of the season.

> *The silk lines used prior to World War II required constant maintenance and care. An untreated silk line would not float. Fly lines had to be "dressed," that is, coated with a dressing and allowed to dry for 15-20 minutes. This process had to be repeated every few hours of fishing, thus contributing to fly fishing's reputation as the "contemplative sport." In England during this period, line dressing and other tackle chores, as well as mixing drinks and preparing lunches, would have been performed by a "gillie," a servant who attended to the aristocratic anglers while they enjoyed their leisure.*

FLY RODS

Prior to about 1850, fly rods were constructed of a solid branch of wood, and were by today's standards extremely heavy. The real breakthrough came with the development of split-cane fly rods. Lengths of cured bamboo were split, and the resulting sections planed to triangle-shaped sections with a specified taper. Six identical sections were thus prepared, then glued together to form a six-sided tapered fly rod section. Three to five such sections, each joined to the next by metal joins, termed "ferrules," were required to complete a fly rod.

Independent craftsmen produced rods of astonishing beauty and delicacy of action. Using the new techniques rods could be built much lighter than before, and using machine tools of that era the craftsman could adjust and refine the tapers to produce the desired action.

During World War II the military developed a wide range of new materials including fiberglass. After the war these new materials and technologies were made available for civilian applications, and one of these was the fiberglass fly rod. Fiberglass could be mass-produced, thus lowering costs. Fiberglass rods tended to have a "faster" action, as described in the next section. Also, a fiberglass rod weighed considerably less than a comparable bamboo rod. Fiberglass decimated the split bamboo market and dominated rod building from 1950 through about 1970, when a new material came on the scene–modular graphite.

Modular graphite was developed by the aerospace industry and, like fiberglass, spawned a host of new recreation-related products. The first graphite rods were sold in the mid-1970s, and within a few years graphite became and has remained the dominant fly rod material. I do not pretend to understand the science behind graphite versus fiberglass materials and the resulting fly rods, and you do not need to understand it either to become a proficient caster. To summarize, a graphite rod can be built much lighter than a comparable fiberglass rod and, because the material is inherently stiffer, the graphite rod's action will tend to be faster; see Rod Action below.

Rod Weight

As we discussed earlier, modern single-handed rods and their lines are rated using the AFTMA system. **The "weight" of the rod does not refer to its physical weight, but the line weight that will properly load the rod**. By "loading" of a rod we mean bending and consequentially storing energy, followed by releasing that energy during casting.

Let's use the analogy of a metal spring: An object to be propelled is placed on a spring. The spring is compressed (loaded). When the spring is released, the stored energy is released and the object is projected through space.

A few points to ponder: A stouter spring will require more weight to load it than one made with thinner metal. Likewise, a heavier rod will require a heavier line to load it.   Also, if insufficient weight is placed on the spring, it will not become fully loaded and therefore project less energy. Likewise, a weight #7 rated fly rod with a weight #4 line will only partially load. *When casting it will feel like trying to throw a feather.*

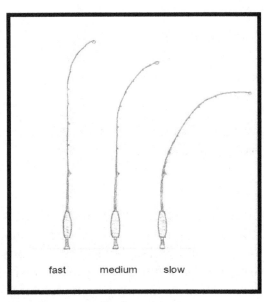

Rod action.

The AFTMA rating for a rod will be stated on the label found on the rod directly above the handle. Many rods are rated for a two-weight band, i.e., "#4-#5."

What happens if you put on a heavier weight line than is needed to load your rod? Nothing much, it will still load and cast, but you will lose the delicacy of presentation and not gain any additional casting distance, and it will feel clumsy.

Rod Action

Rod action is independent of weight and refers to the extent of the rod that bends when fully loaded. A rod that bends mainly at the tip is termed a "fast action" rod, with medium and slow action rods the bending extends progressively further down towards the handle. Graphite rods tend to have the fastest actions, fiberglass slower, and bamboo the slowest of the three.

What does rod action mean to you as a beginning fly-caster?

A slower rod will require a slower, more deliberate casting action as well as tend to cause the line loop to be wider than when casting with a faster rod, as will be explained in Chapter 8, Casting. A wide loop translates into more air resistance thus making long casts more difficult.

Rod action is, to a great extent, a matter of preference. However, slow action rods make forming a tight casting loop difficult; for this reason, I would recommend medium-fast or medium action for your first rod. Casting weighted flies works better with a somewhat slower rod. Fast action rods are difficult for the beginning caster to sense when they are loaded and the forward cast should begin.

Unfortunately, rod action is not normally indicated on the rod label. How do you determine the action? In a store, hopefully the retail staff will know. Here is an important advantage to shopping at a pro shop: They will have the expertise; in a big-box retail store they may or may not. To determine a rod's action one can hold the rod horizontal, lower the tip to the floor, gently push the tip against the carpet and bend the rod. Observe the curve of the rod, note how far down the rod it bends. Compare with other rods.

Rod Care

The modern fly rod requires very little maintenance. With reasonable care one will last a lifetime– or more. However, rods are essentially fragile tools and easily broken if stepped on, run over by a vehicle (I will admit to this one), smashed in a car door, etc. A few years ago, I conducted a scientific survey and determined that 90 percent of experienced anglers have broken a rod in some such manner and the other 10 percent are liars.

For each of my rods I have made an inexpensive case out of PVC drain pipe and have disciplined myself to always store them in the cases. Drill a dozen or so ½-inch holes in the PVC pipe to allow moisture to escape. PVC endcaps can be purchased, and one glued to the pipe and the other removable. Lightweight cotton "socks" to protect the finish on the rod are nice but not essential.

LEADERS

The main purpose of the leader is to put a near-invisible connection between the fish and the fly line. When a fish approaches your fly you don't want him scared by the highly visible fly line. Three hundred sixty years ago, Charles Cotton recommended fishing "fine and far off" to avoid scaring fish.

A leader is a tapered unit, like a fly line; however, it tapers only in one direction, thinning as it approaches the fly. Leaders for floating lines normally range from six to 12 feet or longer, with a nine-foot leader a good starting point for most floating line work.

The leader consists of a butt section, a taper, and a "tippet." The tippet is usually about three feet

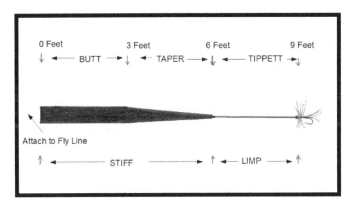

Typical nine-foot tapered leader.

long and is a continuous piece of relatively thin nylon or fluorocarbon tied onto the end of the leader. Why does the leader taper? It is an extension of taper of the line; the taper allows for the energy of the cast to gradually dissipate and gently drop the fly on the water.

Leader material and tippets are measured by diameter using the "X" system, not by breaking strength. Here is the formula: 11 minus the X size always equals the diameter in thousandths of an inch, hence:

4X = 11 minus 4 = .007" diameter

5X = 11 minus 5 = .006" diameter

6X = 11 minus 6 = .005" diameter

The diameter of the tippet is very important because this is what the fish will see, and also is the weakest link, the one most likely to be broken by a fighting fish. Clear water, small flies, a smooth water surface, full sunlight, and educated trout all call for finer tippets. Tippets range from 0X through 7X; I recommend that the beginner use 4X tippet as a basic starting point for most trout fishing. It is a good all-around tippet that is not difficult to work with. The beginner should also be armed with a spool of 5X and 2X as well. The finer tippets, 6X, 7X, etc., are difficult to tie and cast, and I would defer their use until you have fully mastered basic casting and line handling skills.

In the past, leaders were constructed by tying together progressively thinner strands of leader material. Today it is more common to buy leaders that have been chemically tapered (extruded) and thus one continuous piece without knots. To this continuous leader, a tippet of 24" to 36" is tied on with a triple surgeon's knot.

One thing to get used to is that the tippet will need to be replaced and rebuilt over the course of a season several times, while the butt end can stay semi-permanently attached to your fly line. Each time you switch flies, you will lose about 4-6 inches of tippet length. So after changing flies, say, three times on your first trip, your 30" tippet is now about half of its original length. You need to replace the tippet. Short tippets have two disadvantages: (1) they are weaker because there is less length of material to stretch before breaking; and (2) the fish sees more of the thicker leader material.

So you now need to replace that tippet. Chop off the old one at the knot and tie on a new tippet using a triple surgeon's knot. Note that each time you replace or change tippets you are also shortening the taper section. At some point you will need to re-build it as well, or just replace the entire leader.

Another consideration regarding leaders and tippets is the stiffness or limpness of the leader material. Stiffness assists in turning over the fly at the end of the cast. If the cast does not have enough energy the leader will fall onto the water in a pile. But if the leader material is stiff this will help it turn over. Remember that the weight of the fly is an impediment to the leader fully rolling out during a cast. However, once the cast is complete, a stiff tippet will inhibit the motion of the fly in the water. Remember that the things fish eat aren't normally tethered to lengths of nylon and pulled around the water. They float and drift in a natural manner, subject to the stream's subtle currents. A softer, limper tippet will assist in accomplishing this. So, the leader is trying to meet two conflicting goals. The solution usually arrived at is to use stiff material for the butt and the taper portions and soft, pliable material for the tippet. Leader material is readily available in both forms.

HOOKS

Hooks (and flies) are measured by the "gape," which is the distance between the point and the shank of the hook.

Hooks range in size from 2/0 to as small as #24. The smaller the hook, the larger the number; the larger the hook, the smaller the number. Hooks today, are generally sold only in the even numbers, though odd numbers were sold in the past and theoretically exist. As a beginner, you should avoid the extremes–yes, a consistent theme of this book. Sizes between #8 and #14 are good for beginners. Flies smaller than #14 will force you to use finer and finer tippets, which are hard to cast and handle. Larger flies are difficult to cast and won't work well with a #5 or #6 weight outfit.

The "X" System of Relative Length and Thickness

In addition to the gape, hooks are also measured by the relative thickness of the wire used and the relative length of the hook. Each size of hook has a standard wire thickness and shank length. As

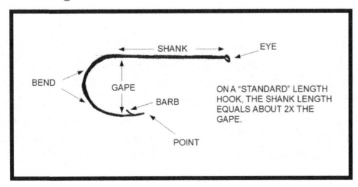

hooks get larger, the standard wire thickness and shank length increase. If the hook is built to the standard length and thickness, it is described by the number only, e.g. "#12." However, a hook described as "#12; *2x Stout*" will be a #12 hook built from thicker wire, that of a standard hook two steps up the scale, a #10 hook. A hook described as "#12; *1X*

Fine" will be made of thinner wire, that of a standard hook one step down the scale, a #13 hook.

Why all this stout and fine complication stuff? Here's why: Dry flies are designed to float. "Fine" hooks weigh less than standard hooks, thus they aid in keeping dry flies afloat. Nymphs are normally intended to sink rapidly thus they are often tied on over-stout hooks.

Relative length works with the same "X" system, e.g., *2x Long, 3x Long,* or *2x Short.* Long hooks are useful for tying streamers designed to imitate small fish. Short hooks are useful for tying egg patterns.

In recent years, barbless hooks have become increasingly popular. They assist with the release of fish and in many waters are legally required. To de-barb a hook, merely flatten the barb with a pair of needle-nose pliers. I have fished barbless exclusively for about twenty years and have no regrets.

Hooks for fly fishing need to be razor sharp. In fly fishing the fish strikes at the fly, quickly recognizes it is bogus, and expels it. In bait fishing the fish takes in the bait and is somewhat slower to notice that, attached to the chow, is the gosh-darn hook. Fly fishers should always carry a small sharpening stone and periodically check hooks for sharpness. Large flies seem to be the ones that need the most sharpening.

Balanced Outfit: Matching Fly Size and Tippet

There is a range of fly sizes that will work a given tippet diameter. **The smaller the fly, the finer the tippet.** If the tippet is too stout, first you may know this because the tippet won't even go through the eye of the hook. If it does you will be able to use it but it won't be optimal – the over-stiff tippet will not allow the fly to swing naturally in the water, and you are basically defeating the purpose of going to a smaller fly.

If the leader/tippet is too fine for the size of fly, two things may happen: (1) you may have trouble tying the fly onto the leader without the knot slipping; and (2) casting will be difficult because the heavy fly won't "turn over" and roll out nicely.

Tippet	Diameter	Fly Size							
		18	16	14	12	10	8	6	4
2x	0.009	X	X	M	M	I	I	I	I
3x	0.008	X	M	M	I	I	I	I	M
4x	0.007	X	M	I	I	I	M	M	M
5x	0.006	M	I	I	I	M	M	X	X
6x	0.005	I	I	I	M	M	X	X	X

I = IDEAL   M = MARGINAL   X = UNWORKABLE

You could, if you had to, fly fish without a reel. I have done it; it's not as hard as fishing without a rod. I'm spending less time covering reels because they are not a critical success factor the way lines, leaders, flies, and rods are.

Reels hold unused line and also aid in playing large fish. While you could theoretically fish without a reel, a proper reel adds to the enjoyment as well as the efficiency of the sport. Reels are sized to match lines as are rods, but not in an exact manner. Most reels sold today will list a range of line sizes that the reel will hold, such as "4/5/6" or "7/8".

Reels come in many styles and prices. For most trout fishing, an inexpensive, serviceable reel will do everything that an expensive reel will do. The expensive reel will probably last longer, though I have my doubts, having recently had a premier, very expensive reel fall apart, un-repairable, after about two years' service.

A bottom-line requirement for a fly reel is a good workable drag system. The drag on a fly reel serves two functions: (1) when a fish is hooked it provides adjustable resistance to the fish's efforts to escape; and (2) it prevents the reel from over-spinning and snarling when line is pulled from the reel.

The drag system on a fly reel may seem anemic to the angler accustomed to spin rods. With a spin rod, thin monofilament line travels through large guides with virtually no resistance. The resistance must be provided entirely by the drag itself. With fly gear, the fly line, ten or twenty times the diameter of the monofilament, passes through smaller guides and this provides considerable resistance. Also, many fly reels have an exposed rim that allows the angler to add additional drag by "palming," i.e., rubbing the palm of his hand on the exposed rim.

Avoid reels that lack an internal drag and rely solely on palming. Note the two purposes of the drag above. The rim control will serve the first purpose but can do nothing to stop the reel from over-spinning, resulting in a snarled mess when you pull line from the reel. I inventoried my reels and found that out of 12 reels that I own, two have no internal drag. I consider these reels unusable.

Drags are of two kinds: the "ratchet and pawl" and the "disk" drag. Ratchet and pawl drags are sometimes called a "click" drag because they produce a click sound as line is paid out. They are found on light and medium duty reels and are entirely adequate for most fly fishing. Disk drags work like a disk brake on a car; two disks are pressed together resulting in adjustable drag. Disk drags are much more powerful than ratchet and pawl and are utilized both for trout reels and for "big game" reels such as saltwater or salmon fishing reels.

Most drags are adjustable. Generally, there will be a dial of some kind on the reel face; turning it clockwise increases the drag; counter-clockwise reduces it–usually. I own one reel that works the opposite direction. Oh well!

Care and maintenance of reels

With a little periodic maintenance and reasonable care, a decent fly reel should last for decades. Your reel will need an occasional squirt of machine oil on the spindle and other moving parts. Periodically, depending on use and the amount of dirt you encounter, you should take the reel apart, clean it with a mild soap and water, thoroughly dry it and re-lube all of the moving parts.

Sand is the arch-enemy of reels. Keep your reel out of the sand if at all possible.

Reel Backing

If you omitted backing and just put your 90-foot fly line onto the reel, it would work, but most of the spool would be empty, and reeling in line would be much slower due to the smaller diameter of each revolution of the reel handle. So, line or reel backing is first spooled onto the reel to take up the space, then the line on top of the backing.

A second reason for backing is when a large or very feisty fish is hooked and runs with wild abandon, pulls out the entire 90-foot fly line and still wants to run more. A new fly angler's first fish that pulls line off the reel and runs into the backing should remain fondly in memory.

Backing is usually made of braided Dacron. Depending on its size, a reel will hold about 50-100 yards of backing, plus the fly line. To determine the right amount of backing, you can reel the fly line on first, then fill the reel with backing, then unspool everything onto a coffee can, then wind it all back on in the correct order. It sounds like a lot of work but the result will be the correct amount of backing. When you do this, be sure not to fill the reel all the way to the brim with backing. Leave a little space– just enough to insert your finger between the top of the line and the outer rim of the reel–for margin of error so that if the line isn't wound back on as tight as possible there will still be room. If you run out of room retrieving line, the line will bind against the reel frame and refuse to move. This will probably happen with that big fish of your dreams on the line.

KNOTS

A wide variety of knots can be used to assemble your rod and reel. I am describing the knots that I have come to use and trust; other experienced anglers may use other knots and recommend them to you. That's fine. **There is more than one way to fly fish**.

The triple surgeon's knot and the improved clinch knot (or some equivalent) are used every time you fish. You should practice these two at home until you can do them in your sleep. You will be tying these knots under less than ideal conditions: when your hands are ice-cold, when it is nearly dark, when fish are jumping all around you, or all three at once!

The knots joining the fly and tippet and the tippet to the leader are typically the weak links in the entire outfit, the first to break, therefore it is essential to tie these knots properly. **Always, always, test each newly tied knot before you cast.** I formed this habit years ago, and each year, once or twice, I will tie a knot, give it a good, strong pull, and have it promptly unravel.

Triple Surgeon's Knot

This is the basic knot I use to tie the tippet to the leader, or tie together tapering sections of leader material. It will hold fast even if the two pieces are of different diameters. For this reason, I use it to tie on tippets as well as re-build leaders. Some fly fishermen use the blood knot to build leaders, but I do not. I find it more difficult to tie, and it is reliable only if the two leader sections are of similar diameter.

Step #1: Lay the two stands to be joined next to each other; the overlap needs to be at least 6- 8 inches.

Step #2: Twist the two sections as a unit to form a loop.

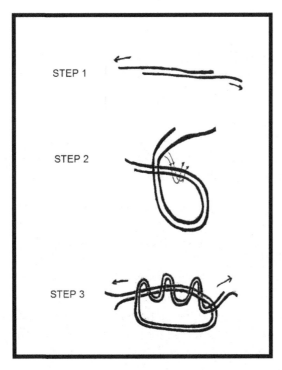

Triple Surgeon's Knot

Step #3: Pass the two sections that point towards the fly end through this loop three times.

Step #4: Grab the two upper pieces with one hand and both lower pieces with the other hand, wet the knot with saliva, and pull all four pieces tight.

Step #5: Snip off the two ends that are left. Double-check first to see if you have the right ends that are not to be used. I have tied this knot for 35 years and each year once or twice I snip off the wrong end. Oh well! If you do this, return to step #1 and start over.

The purpose of wetting the knot with saliva before you draw it tight is to lubricate the nylon to prevent friction that will overheat and damage the material. This is a good habit to get into when tying any fishing knot.

Improved Clinch Knot

This is a simple yet highly effective knot for attaching fly to tippet.

Pass the tippet through the eye of the fly then twirl the end around the standing portion of the tippet 5 or 6 times. Then pass the end through the space formed by the line closest to the eye. Then pass the end through the resulting space. Wet the knot, draw it tight, and snip off the tag end.

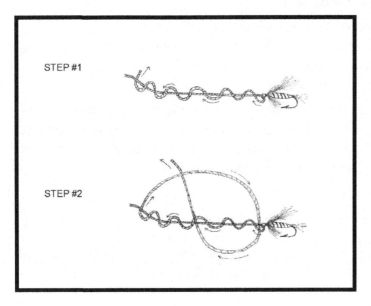

Improved clinch knot.

Putting it all together: Assembling your Six-weight Balanced Fly Rod

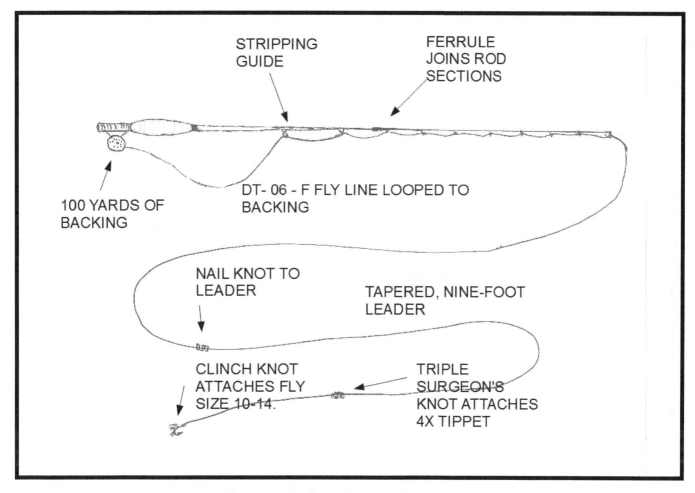

A typical six-weight fly rod assembled and ready to fish.

Assembling the Reel, Backing, and Fly Line

The direction you should spool on the backing and line depends on whether you cast right-handed or left-handed.

I have always casted left-handed and always will, but I don't have anything against casting right-handed. It is just like handwriting; over the years I have known many people who write right-handed and they seem to do OK.

Just to prove my lack of prejudice I have presented all of the casting directions assuming a right-handed caster.

The line needs to be spooled onto the reel so that when mounted on the rod, the line leads away from the bottom of the reel, not the top.

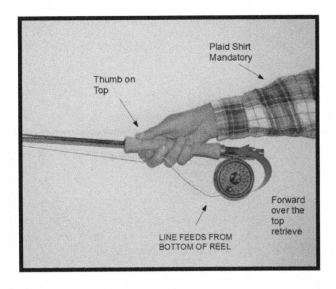

Another way to describe the proper line spooling is that when you are reeling in line you are reeling forward over the top of the reel. This is true for either a right- or left hander.

A right-hander will cast with the right hand, and reel in line with the left hand, and the reverse for a left-hander. An older method, still used by a few today, calls for switching hands and using one's dominant hand for both casting and reeling. It is rarely taught today and can be safely ignored.

Joining Reel and Backing

The backing is tied to the reel using the simple arbor knot illustrated below.

Joining Backing and Fly Line

I join the backing and fly line by making an improved end loop (see below) at the end of the fly line, and then tying the backing to it via a clinch knot.

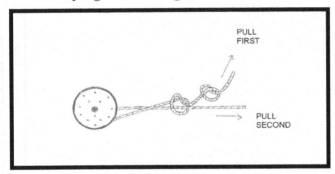

Arbor knot.

Joining Fly line and Leader

Two different systems are popular.: the nail knot and the loop-to-loop.

The nail knot provides a semi-permanent, extremely strong connection. Being a rigid connection, the leader turns over with no loss of energy from fly line to leader. The nail knot is a little tricky to tie and involves using a small tool available at a tackle store. When you buy a new line and leader at a pro shop, if you ask them they will usually join the two with a nail knot for you. If they won't, find a new pro shop.

After the knot is tied, I usually coat it with nail polish or some other coating material such as "Pliobond." This results in a smooth surface that will not snag if the line brushes against a tree branch, the other end of the leader, or your shirt. Incidentally, coating any semi-permanent connection in this manner is a good idea.

So what's not to like about the nail knot connection? *You cannot change leaders while out fishing.* You may or may not want to change leaders while fishing. For me, what I change in and out of is sinking leaders. I discovered sinking leaders a few years ago and use them to get a wet fly down a few inches to a few feet easily without switching to a sink-tip or a sinking line. But just as quick as I want to put it on, I may need to take it off. For this reason, I reluctantly migrated from the nail knot to the loop-to -loop. Another leader-switching scenario is that many nymph anglers like to use specialized nymph leaders. If you don't anticipate needing to switch leaders, then the nail knot connection is best.

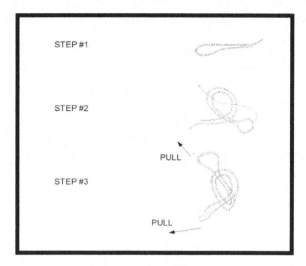

STEP #1

STEP #2

PULL

STEP #3

PULL

Improved end loop.

The loop-to-loop connection allows for quick, easy swapping from one leader to another. It has two notable disadvantages. One is that it does not transfer the energy of the cast seamlessly from line through to the leader as does the nail knot. This is because the connection is "loose," or "hingy." The second disadvantage is that the resulting connection is much more prone to getting hung up in the guides.

To make the loop-to-loop connection, a loop is needed at the ends of both the line and leader. Some leaders and lines come with a pre-tied loop. If not, I use the improved end loop described above. If the line does not come with a pre-tied loop, you may want to nail-knot a short length of .030" leader material to the end of the line, then tie an improved end loop in the other end. The reason for this is that the end loop in the .030" leader will be smaller than one tied in the fly line itself. An improved end loop tied in the end of a fly line results in a sizable bump that will catch on the guides.

The resulting loop-to-loop connection, when complete, should look like a Boy Scout square knot—it should be symmetrical.

Increasingly today, fly lines are constructed with a built-in loop. With these, just tie an end loop in your leader and join as described above.

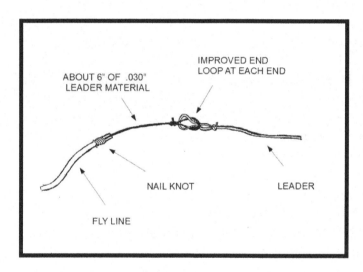

IMPROVED END
LOOP AT EACH END

ABOUT 6" OF .030"
LEADER MATERIAL

NAIL KNOT

LEADER

FLY LINE

Loop-to-loop connection.

Joining Leader and Tippet

Join with the triple surgeon's knot described earlier.

Threading the Line through the Guides

A little trick to make this easier: Take the line near where it joins the leader and bend it back over itself, forming what boating types call a "bight." The end of this bight is then pushed through the guides. This makes it easier to handle, and prevents the line from falling back down through the guides if you accidentally let go of it. When you get it through the tip-top guide, pull enough line out so that the end of the tippet is down near the handle. When fishing, you should never reel in your line beyond that point.

A few inches above the handle many rods have a "fly keeper," a small ring or length of wire attached to the rod similar to a guide. This is NOT a guide and the fly line does not thread through it on its way up the rod. When you have threaded the line through each guide and tied on a fly, hook the fly through this fly keeper. It will hold the line in place as you hike to your fishing spot or when you set the rod down to take a break.

Before you fish, double check that the line is threaded through each and every guide. Missing any guide will allow the line to wrap around the rod and prevent the line from moving. The kiss of death.

Now tie on the fly and you are ready to fish.

Joining Tippet and Fly

My basic knot between fly and tippet is the improved clinch knot, but there are other alternatives: the Duncan loop provides a loose, yet strong connection that allows the fly to wiggle and meander laterally; the double turle knot makes a direct connection to the shank of the hook, thus ensuring that the fly swims directly in line with the leader. These are refinements that you may or may not choose to pursue. Salt-water fly fishing employs its own unique knots.

Avoid:

- Fly/spin "combo" rods. Designed to function as either a fly rod or a spin-casting rod, they do neither well. They cast like an old broom.
- "Automatic" fly reels. The user depresses a lever at the base of the fly reel, and line is sucked up onto the reel. These reels are expensive, complicated, and heavy. A solution in search of a problem.
- Level fly lines. Lacking a taper at the end of the line, the line tends to slap the water instead of gently rolling out onto the water.
- Bamboo, for the wrong reasons. Many folks collect, repair, fish with, and even build bamboo rods, and enjoy these hobbies immensely. But don't go out a get a bamboo rod because you were told by an "expert" that all the "best" fly fishermen fish with bamboo exclusively, or any such nonsense.
- Tiny one or two weight micro rods. Not for your first rod.
- Reels with only a rim "palm" drag. Unless you thoroughly enjoy straightening out snarled lines.
- Brightly colored fly lines. Stick to natural, drab colors.
- Hip waders and boot-footed waders. These are acceptable for a sandy-bottomed river but are not up to the job on slippery rocks.

7. Other Gear

- **Vests:** Fly fishers typically are highly mobile while fishing thus don't want to lug around a tackle box. The solution is the fishing vest with multiple pockets which frees both hands to fish and eliminates the need to wade to shore to retrieve a tackle box.
- **Fly floatant:** Floatant repels water and thus aids in floating a dry fly. Sold in liquid and spray formats.
- **Line cleaner:** Sold in a tube; I squirt some onto a rag and run the line through the rag. Helps keep the line supple and clean.
- **Reel lube:** Just a drop on the reel's spindle and other moving parts will prolong the life of a reel.
- **Needle-nose pliers:** Handy for crimping down the barbs on flies, removing a fly from a fish's mouth, and a variety of other situations.
- **Nail clippers:** Not for pedicure needs, but rather to snip off the ends of leader material after tying knots. These are so handy I usually carry two pair.
- **Small folding pocket knife:** For field dressing a fish, and other outdoorsy tasks. Also useful for whittling a stick while you sit in your car at 7:30 AM waiting for your fishing partner to finish getting his gear and coffee ready when you agreed to leave at 7AM.
- **Sharpening stone:** Keep your hooks sticky sharp! In my experience the larger or stouter hooks require the most sharpening.
- **Polarized sunglasses:** Primarily for eye safety, but also to aid in observing below the water's surface.
- **Rain gear:** Don't leave home without it.
- **Landing net:** Handy especially when fishing from a boat. I try to avoid carrying one when wading because it's seems to be in the way all the time. Just my personal preference.
- **Flashlight and spare batteries:** "Just one more cast; there's still plenty of light." Yeah, right. What self-respecting fly fisher hasn't been in this situation? There may be light for that one last cast, but there is still the hike through the dark forest back to your vehicle. An essential safety tool. Another safety tool is a whistle–it can summon help better than a human voice and carries over longer distances. Attach it to your vest.
- **Wading equipment:**
  - **Waders** have come a long way since I started fly fishing 35 years ago. I have a photo of a group of expert fly fishermen from the 1950s, and many were wearing the old boot-built-into-the-rubber-waders style. These might be OK for a sandy-bottom river but for most river wading *they are totally inadequate.* I had a pair in the early 1980s, but soon graduated to stocking foot waders, which is the only way to go. Modern stocking foot waders come in two basic types: (1) neoprene. These help keep you warm in cold weather; and (2) breathable. Much more comfortable in warm weather. Waders are not cheap and since they won't last as long as a fly rod, **they may be your most expensive item**. Waders must be treated

carefully or you will not even get one season out of them. Barb-wire fences, blackberry bushes, etc., can rip your waders to shreds. My experience is that with proper care I can get perhaps three years' service from a good pair.

- **Wading boots** lace up and support your ankles as well as provide traction on the river bottom. Traction is essential in our swift, rocky, Pacific Northwest rivers. Some boots come with felt soles, others rely on either built-in or strap-on traction devices. Currently I am using a pair of slip-on metal cleats. Don't attempt to wade without adequate traction.
- **Wading staff.** An essential safety tool. My simple approach: To a chest-height, wooden walking stick, I attach a lanyard that can snap on or off my belt. When not in use, I can leave it attached to the belt and swing it over my shoulder out of way. Although many anglers prefer foldable wading staffs, they are marketed at, from my perspective, exorbitant prices, with questionable utility. They have the advantage of being out of the way when not in use.
- **Belt.** A stout belt around the outside of your waders will keep out water if you fall in. Most waders include such a belt. Be sure to wear it!

- **Hats:** In most jurisdictions in the United States it is illegal to fly fish without wearing a hat. Or so it would seem based on we anglers' penchant for cranium-based sartorial self-expression. Good, clean fun, but a hat also performs important functions for the angler: it shields the sun from your eyes, keeps the rain off your head, and stops the loss of body heat. As any outdoor-person knows, you lose most of your body heat from your head, not your fingers or toes. A suitable hat must have a bill or brim to keep the sun out of your eyes and off your face. I greatly dislike fishing without a hat.
- **Insect repellent**.
- **Small repair kit.** I put together a small tool kit I find useful anytime I am out of doors. Remember that you may be a long way from any help. I include: pliers, duct tape, WD-40, screwdriver, wader repair kit, thin twine or wire, spare batteries, spare parts for my pontoon boat, and a magnifying glass.

8. Casting

Fly casting is, for many people, fly fishing's most distinctive aspect. When done well, it is both enjoyable to watch and satisfying to execute. The rhythmic forward and back motion creates an enveloping calm.

Fly casting is a skill that can be learned by practice and a thorough grasp of a few basic principles. It does not require extraordinary strength, coordination, or other athletic prowess. Once the basics are mastered, advanced skills can be developed through experience.

Practice, practice, practice. You can practice on a lawn or in a nearby park but not on a street or other hard surface because this will strip the finish off a good fly line in a matter of minutes. But better than a lawn is a nearby pond. As a bonus, the pond may likely host panfish, which are great for fly fishing.

Nice tight-looped cast! Carol Kohler works through a fine drift on Washington's Lewis River. Photo by John Geyer.

Rod Loading Defined

Rod loading refers to the fly rod bending from the weight of the line in motion and thus storing energy. In this respect a fly rod is like a spring or an archery bow. All three of these tools store energy as they are loaded, then release all the energy at a single point in time. In the case of the archery bow, energy is stored as the archer draws back the arrow; when the arrow is released the stored energy is also released. With the fly rod, the energy is stored by accelerating the line (see Step 3 below). The stored energy is released by the **Hard Stop**.

To demonstrate this principle another way, take a rod mounted with reel and floating line and extend beyond the rod tip about twenty feet of line plus a tapered leader, and attach a barbless fly. Have a friend hold the rod horizontal. You hold the fly and walk away from your friend, perpendicular to the rod, straightening out the line. When the line is straight, keep walking until the rod bends sharply. The rod at this point is fully loaded. The energy is stored. Let go of the fly and watch the rod cast itself.

This is what people mean when they say "let the rod do the work."

THE OVERHEAD CAST

All directions in this chapter, as in the entire book, assume a right-handed angler.

Basic Stance

Pretend you are playing catch with your 10-year-old daughter or nephew. You will take a stance with your left toe about 20 inches in front of your right toe with both pointing generally in the direction of your toss. Your knees will be bent slightly. Your right hand will hold the ball and be held slightly in front of you. Your weight will be on your left foot. You will reach back with your right arm, leaning back, putting your weight on your right foot. Then you will throw the ball while shifting your weight forward, ending with your weight on your left foot and your right toe just touching the ground with no weight on it.

The basic stance for fly casting is the same.

It is important in fly casting that your right-hand grip the rod with your **thumb on top.** This helps prevent your rod from traveling back too far in step 3 below, and thus helps you form a tight loop.

Step by Step

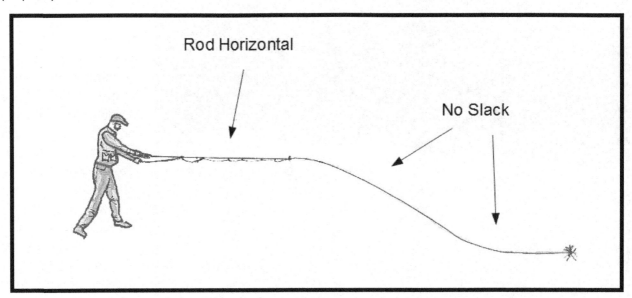

1. Get Set: Basic stance as described above. The fly rod is pointing straight towards the line and the line does not have slack anywhere. If there is slack, strip the line in until the slack is gone before casting. This is critical. If there are loose coils of line in front of the rod or anywhere, when you cast you will pick up the slack and the fly will not move. If the fly does not move you are not casting. Your left hand is holding the line. You should have about 25 feet of line in front of you.

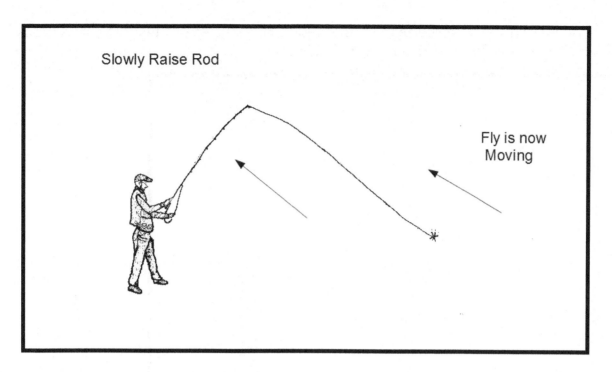

Slowly Raise Rod

Fly is now Moving

2. Lift Rod: To begin the back cast, slowly move your right hand toward your right ear. The line and fly should begin to lift off the water. Your forearm should be doing the casting, not your wrist. As you move your arm back, gradually shift your weight to your back foot.

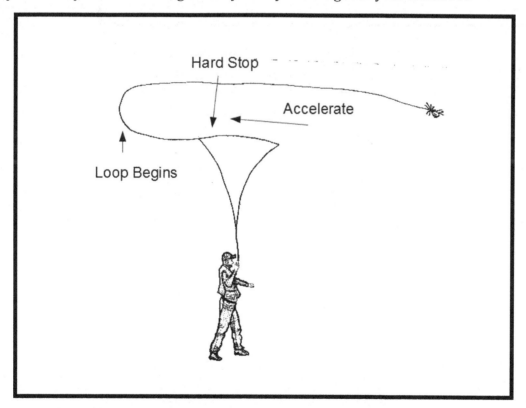

Hard Stop

Accelerate

Loop Begins

3. Accelerate and STOP: Now begin to accelerate and keep accelerating until the rod reaches the 12 o'clock position, then make an abrupt **Hard Stop**. This abrupt stop is what causes the rod to unload like a spring being released. It also causes the line to form a loop. DON'T LET THE ROD

TRAVEL BEYOND THE 12 o'clock POSITION BEFORE THE STOP. At this point the backcast is complete and your weight should be on your right foot.

4. Wait and Drift: Now you need to WAIT as the line loop unrolls behind you. While waiting, let the rod drift back to about 2 o'clock. When do you start the forward cast? When the line has completely straightened out behind you, start the forward cast.

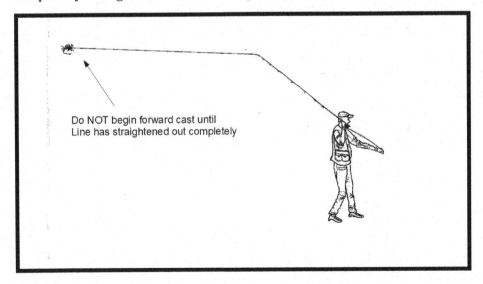

Do NOT begin forward cast until
Line has straightened out completely

5. Start Forward: The forward cast is virtually identical to the backcast. When the line is straight behind you, start moving your rod hand forward, slowly at first, then accelerate. Transfer your weight from your back leg to your forward leg.

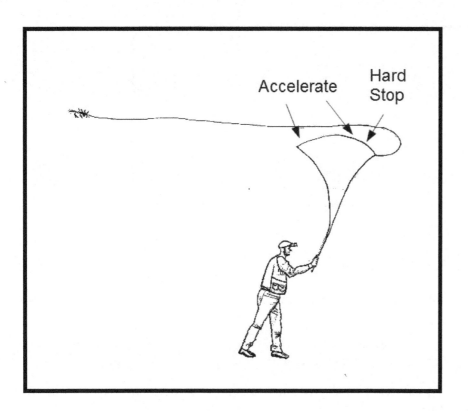

6. Accelerate and STOP: When the rod is at 12 o'clock, make an abrupt **Hard Stop**.

7. Drift and Point: The line is now unrolling forward. Drift the rod forward and point it a few feet above the surface of the water in the direction you are casting.

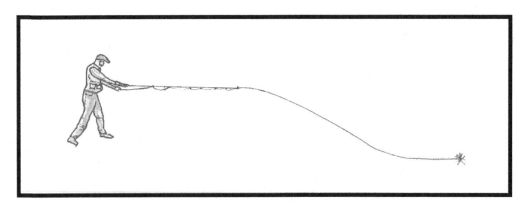

8. End: Watch the line roll out onto the water with your rod horizontal, ready to begin fishing.

THREE CORNERSTONES OF A GOOD CAST

1. **Develop a tight loop by making a Hard Stop and not letting your wrist drop back during the power stroke.**

   Learning to cast a tight loop is **Goal Numero Uno** for the beginning caster. A wide or non-existent loop causes the line to lack momentum and the cast to be short and powerless.

   What is the "Power Stroke"? The Power Stroke is the arc made by the rod tip during the acceleration up to the **Hard Stop**.

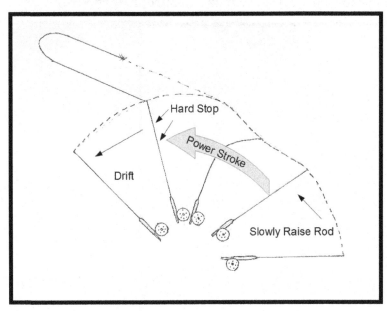

Good tight loop.

The size of the loop is determined by the path the rod tip takes during the Power Stroke. A wide arc taken by your rod tip will result in a wide loop, slow line speed and a weak, short cast. A narrow arc will result in a tighter loop, greater line speed, and a better cast. Notice that the loop has upper and lower legs. The lower leg, where the loop begins, always starts at the location of the rod tip when the Hard Stop occurs. The upper leg is determined by the highest point the rod tip traveled during the Power Stroke. Don't use your wrist when you cast, use your arm. Keep your wrist locked. Another aid to a tight loop is to use the thumb on top hand position.

The "roundhouse" cast is caused by dropping the wrist back during the power stroke, thereby widening the power stroke as well as the loop. A cast with a wide loop simply won't have any momentum.   Like a roundhouse punch thrown by a drunken sailor in a Tijuana bar, a roundhouse cast is consistently ineffective.

2. **Start the cast with the rod horizontal and no slack line between the rod tip and the fly.** See step 1 above. The fly must move as soon as you begin the cast, not later. Also, be sure to have a good grip on the fly line with your left hand. See the illustration below titled "Stripping line."

3. **Don't start the forward cast until the line has fully straightened out behind you.** How to know when it's straight? Turn your head around and watch the line roll out. Do this for a while until you can tell by feel. If you start the forward cast too early you may hear a "snap" and the fly could possibly snap right off the leader. (I've done this many times.)

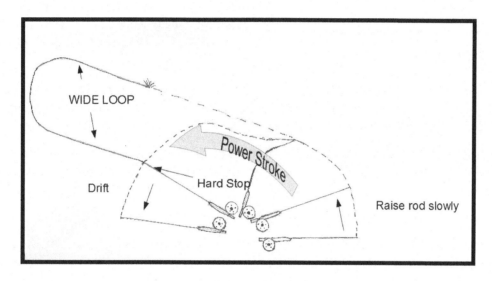

Roundhouse cast. Don't do this!

STRIPPING IN AND SHOOTING LINE

You will want to strip in any loose line and reduce the length of the line to about 25-30 feet to be ready for casting. You may also strip in line during the presentation of the fly, such as when imitating a swimming baitfish. The proper hand position and motion is pictured below:

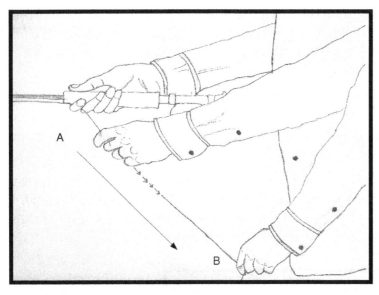

Stripping line.

The right-hand grips the rod with the thumb on top. The line is held against the rod handle by the index finger and runs between the index and middle finger. Strip in line by gripping the line with your left hand at point A above and pulling the line down as far as possible, to point B.

At this point, there are two options. First option is to drop the line and return your left hand to point A. Repeat the stripping motion until the line is in to desired point. With this option the line will fall to your feet or to the floor of your boat.

The second option is to form loops and keep the loops in your left hand. To do this, at point B, don't drop the line, instead carry it with you to point A, grab the line at point A and strip it down, then just repeat until the desired amount of line is in front of you.

Casters usually "shoot line" which means feeding extra line from the loops in your left hand into the cast, lengthening the cast. By shooting line, you can cast further without trying to pick up a long length of line off the water.

To shoot line, you need to have a cast with reasonably good line speed, as explained above.

 The timing of the release of the line is critical. Step 7, above, is the time to shoot line, not before. You must wait until after the **Hard Stop** in the forward cast. Wait until you see the line unrolling in front of you, then release the line from your left hand into the cast. The momentum of the line should draw the line through the guides and into the cast. If it does not, you don't have sufficient line speed to shoot line. Work on getting a nice tight loop and good line speed, then try it again.

After shooting line you may need to strip in line in preparation for the next cast, otherwise you will be attempting to lift too much line off the water. As your casting skills increase you will be able to handle longer lengths of line directly off the water, but for now let's not make it more difficult.

It's also possible to shoot line into the cast during the backcast and during false casts. To keep it simple, limit the shooting of line until the final forward cast. In any case, the principle of waiting until the **Hard Stop** has occurred is critical.

FALSE CASTING

False casting consists of multiple back and forward casts without letting the line and fly touch down on the water at the end of the forward cast. Kind of like a touch and go airplane landing without the touch. Instead of letting the fly land on the water at the end of the forward cast, aim a little higher, and when the fly line is fully unwound in front of you, begin a new back cast.

Why? Several potential purposes:

- For practice; a great way to perfect your stroke

- When fishing a dry fly, to help dry off the fly

- To change the direction of the fly line–see below

False Casting, the Casting Plane and Changing Direction

Another concept: the Casting Plane. To visualize this, imagine a 4-foot by 8-foot piece of plywood standing vertical and lengthwise on the ground forming a plane in the direction you want to cast. You need to maintain the casting plane, i.e., the fly line needs to move along the plane formed by the plywood, with the backcast and the forward cast 180 degrees from each other, not heading off in a different angle.

However, if this were 100 percent true, how could you ever change the direction of the fly line? You would be stuck casting in the same direction all day long. The truth is, you can change directions, just not too much on any single backcast/ forward cast.

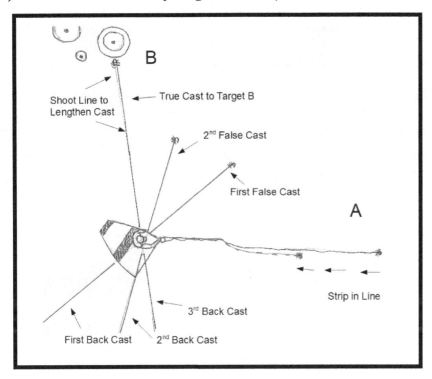

Let's look at an angler fishing a lake from a car-top boat. He is casting and retrieving his line to point A. He has been observing some surface activity at point B and wants to cast there. It is over 90 degrees away. If he tries to back cast, then forward cast to point B, the line will not straighten out and the cast will be a mess. So, he needs to see-saw his way using two false casts then the final "true" cast. First, he strips in line to shorten the line. Then, on the final cast he shoots line to reach the target B. Remember this is much easier to perform with a short line. You can also do an extra false cast at the end if the line is not straightening out properly.

THE ROLL CAST

The roll cast is useful when obstructions behind the angler interfere with a backcast. I find it easy and relaxing to perform. The line never moves more than a couple feet behind the angler. Another purpose is to bring the line to the surface if you are fishing with a sink-tip or full-sinking line.

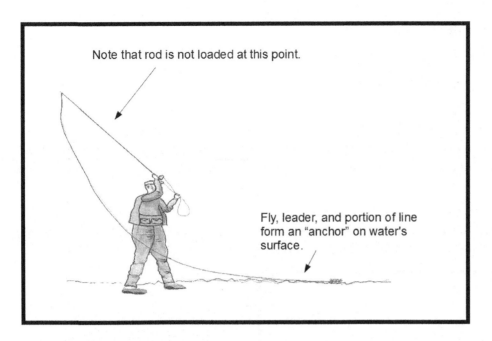

Note that rod is not loaded at this point.

Fly, leader, and portion of line form an "anchor" on water's surface.

1. **Lift Rod Without Accelerating and stop at one o'clock.** An advantage of the roll cast is that the line does not need to be straight out in front of you to start this cast. The fly, leader, and a portion of the line should be on the surface of the water. This "anchor" creates drag on the line and helps load the rod in the next step.

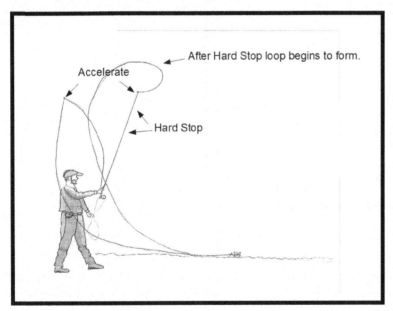

After Hard Stop loop begins to form.

Accelerate

Hard Stop

2. **Slowly begin the forward cast, then accelerate and STOP.** Note that the acceleration and **Hard Stop** powers both this cast as well as the overhead cast. Be sure to make this **Hard Stop** at about 11 o'clock and do not power the rod down to the water.

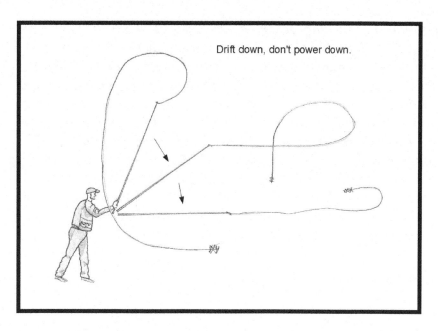

Drift down, don't power down.

3. Drift Forward and Point. You should be watching the loop roll forward now. The unrolling loop is a very different shape than that of the overhead cast. The loop should form a closed oval, then morph into an open loop as in the overhead cast.

Once you have executed the **Hard Stop** and are drifting the rod down, you can shoot line into the cast, just as with an overhead cast.

Many anglers use a roll cast to straighten out the line in preparation for a regular overhead cast. To do this, execute a roll cast as above, but make it a false roll cast by aiming a little higher, then proceed directly to your overhead backcast without letting the line touch down on the water.

Developing Your Casting Skills: Windy Conditions

Sooner or later, you are going to encounter windy weather. You may begin to feel that your hard-earned casting skills have abandoned you at your time of need. Being able to cast under windy conditions is very important. In the places I fish, it seems to be windy most of the time. Here are some ideas to consider:

- The wind usually does not blow consistently everywhere on a lake or stream. Look for protection from the wind in the form of a hill, cliff, or large trees. Sometimes moving 50-100 yards one way or the other will result in considerably less wind.

- The wind usually is reduced closer to the ground and surface of the water as opposed to higher in the air. A sidearm cast can help keep the line down below the wind. To perform the sidearm cast, you are going to tilt the casting plane to the right, away from you, to a nearly horizontal position. Then just make an overhead cast as you normally do.

- In many situations, the wind gusts and then falls calm over a period of 20-30 seconds or so. Simply wait for the lull, then cast.

- A tight loop cuts through the wind much better than a wide loop.

- Don't be a perfectionist. Sometimes all you can do is, by hook or crook, slap the line out there. If it is very windy the surface of the water will be broken and this will help hide a less than perfect cast.

One of my most memorable days fishing occurred at Rocky Ford Creek in Eastern Washington. This spring-fed creek hosts huge rainbows averaging 17-18 inches and is reserved for fly fishing only and catch and release. The March day began at 30 degrees and frost but with an encouraging, warming sun. Later in the morning, clouds formed, the wind freshened, and it began to snow. The snow was so hard I could not see more than 20 yards. I headed to my car for protection and noticed fishermen loading their cars and heading home. In 30 minutes the snow stopped, the sun came out, and within a few minutes I had hooked several rainbows in the 17-20-inch range. Later in the afternoon it began to hail so hard that I sat in my car watching the ground turn white. When the hail stopped, the fishing picked up again. Twice large rainbows stripped out my entire fly line and backing, leaving me helplessly watching as the 5X leader snapped when the reel reached the end of the backing. Later I landed several rainbows well over 20 inches.

If I had given up and left, I would have missed some great fishing.

9. Wild Trout and Their Environment

Awild trout is a beautiful creature that lives in beautiful places. Its sleek shape, wary habits, and strong fighting ability all make it worthy of respect.

In many peoples' minds, trout and fly fishing are mutually joined. And it would be hard to find a better match of quarry to technique. Trout feed on all manner of aquatic insects for which specific flies have been crafted to imitate. At times, in pursuit of these insects, trout will rise to the surface of a stream or lake thus placing themselves in reasonable reach of an angler's fly. When caught on light fly tackle they fight hard, often jumping and running.

I am not a biologist nor trained in the natural sciences; I write this as a layman with the goal of communicating the basics of trout biology and hopefully sparking a desire on the part of the reader for further study. For the material in this chapter I am indebted to Bill Willers's fine book, *Trout Biology, A Natural History of Trout and Salmon*. (See Chapter 20, *For Further Reading*, for additional information about this book.)

Wild versus Native versus Hatchery Trout

Wild trout are defined as the progeny of naturally-spawning adult trout, as opposed to hatchery-raised trout.

Native trout are defined as any species of trout in a given location that have existed there since before man's intervention. Hence a brown trout that grew from an egg buried in the gravel by a spawning female in a stream in Colorado would be a wild trout but not a native trout, because brown trout never existed in America until introduced from Europe in 1883.

Hatchery trout are, obviously, trout reared in a hatchery then released, either as fingerlings or as catchable trout, into a stream or lake.

Taxonomy: The Salmonids

The English word *salmon* is derived from the Latin verb *salire*, "to leap or jump."

The three "true" trout–rainbow, brown, and cutthroat–belong to a family of fish called *salmonids* that also includes Pacific salmon, Atlantic salmon, char, and other groups.

Salmonids are cold-water, fresh-water fish that lack spiny rays. Please review Appendix 1, which outlines, in simplified form, the current biological taxonomy of the salmonids.

Many are surprised by the position of the rainbow and cutthroat trout on the chart. The traditional classification system used by the scientific community prior to 1989 grouped all the trout, along with Atlantic salmon, in the genus *Salmo*. The *Oncorhynchus* genus included only the Pacific salmons. Pacific salmon all spawn once, then within a few days die. Rainbows and cutthroats, like all members of the Salmo genus, can survive spawning and potentially spawn multiple time. Shouldn't all the trouts be together?

The new classification system established in 1989 re-classified the rainbow and cutthroat trout from the *Salmo* genus to the *Oncorhynchus* genus. It reflects biologists' current understanding of the evolution of, and relationship between, the several species. One way to understand the new classification is to note that it is more geographical: *Oncorhynchus* includes all the salmons and trout native to the western region of North America, while all species of the *Salmo* genus hail from either Europe or the East Coast of North America.

Taxonomy: Species and Subspecies

Taxonomy is the biologists' system of classification of living organisms. A *species* is a basic unit of taxonomy. As biologist define the term, it represents a population of individuals that resemble each other and can interbreed.

The term *subspecies* is less well defined. Some biologists recognize many trout subspecies while others classify these as merely "races" or "strains."

Taxonomy: "Races," "Runs," and "Strains"

Certain species display an impressive tendency to diversify throughout their native range; the cutthroat and the rainbow trout are excellent examples. Through natural selection, a given species will evolve to better thrive in its local environment.

A stark example of this can be found in rivers that contain an impassible waterfall. As will be discussed later, rainbows in a stream have a strong instinct to migrate to a larger body of water. Some individuals possess this genetic quality more than others. Those reared below the falls will typically evolve to carry out this urge and migrate to a lake or to the ocean and return back to spawn, if such environment is available. Above the waterfall, those that migrate downstream may flourish elsewhere but they cannot return to spawn in the upper gene pool. Thus over time, natural selection results in a distinct "race" or "strain" residing above the falls that does not migrate downstream.

Less dramatic examples of natural selection and biological diversity can be found wherever trout thrive. Sometimes the differences can be observed by the angler admiring the captured fish, but usually the genetic differences are hidden.

Trout also change their coloration to match their surroundings to aid in protection from predators. For this reason, trout found in rivers tend to be more highly colored than those in lakes, where they take on a silvery hue.

Life History Strategies

Life history strategies refer to the diverse ways in which trout exploit the aquatic habitat available to them.

In some streams a *resident trout* race will spend their entire life in that stream or creek, never moving more than a few hundred yards from their place of birth. In other streams, trout may drop down to a lake to spend all or part of the year feeding, returning to their natal stream to spawn. These trout are termed *adfluvial.* Some races of trout may migrate down from a creek to a larger river. When sexually mature, all trout return to their natal stream to spawn.

Streams open to the ocean may have one or more races of trout, termed *anadromous*, that migrate to salt water, feed for a period that ranges from a few months to several years, then return to spawn.

Anadromous trout, upon reaching about seven inches in length, undergo physical changes termed *smoltification*. These include a change in coloration. The juvenile parr marks and heavy coloration are replaced by a silver tinge on their flanks that will help them hide in their new marine environment. They begin to migrate downstream, and as they pass from fresh water to the brackish water of the estuary their bodies adjust to increased salinity. At this point they are termed "smolts." Some races will continue their downstream migration into the open ocean while others, coastal cutthroat in particular, tend to forage in the estuaries and brackish lower rivers and may never reach the open ocean.

Whether a trout has migrated to the open ocean, a lake, a larger downstream river, or has remained all its life in its natal stream, when the spawning urge beckons, it returns to the *specific portion* of the natal stream where it was born. This is termed **parent stream homing**. This behavior is mind-boggling: A steelhead out-migrates from a lower Columbia River tributary in spring, migrates as far as the Aleutian Islands in Alaska, spends two years foraging, then finds the mouth of the Columbia, then the mouth of its tributary, then returns to that exact spot along that tributary where it was born. Scientists do not fully understand how fish do this, but once the fish reaches the mouth of the river the olfactory sense organs kick in. The olfactory sense organs can detect dissolved substances in concentrations as low as one part in 3,000,000,000,000,000,000. As a juvenile fish, the smell of the gravel of the substrate at its birthplace became implanted in the fish's memory. Now, as a returning adult, it can locate the exact river location of its birth by the smell of the river gravel.

Parent stream homing allows for the evolution of the location-specific strains of each trout species.

Streams open to the salt water may host multiple strains or runs of the same species that return to the natal stream at different times of the year or return to different portions of the stream. Such runs are normally named according to the time of year of their return to the stream, not the season of their spawning. For example, summer-run steelhead, a migratory rainbow, return from salt water to their natal stream anytime from May through October, but do not spawn until the following spring.

Some rivers are blessed with resident trout as well as anadromous races of the same species. Oregon's famed Deschutes River is one of these. Resident rainbows, locally termed "redsides," remain and feed all year on abundant caddis, mayfly and stonefly hatches, and average a robust 12-16 inches at maturity. From nearby river gravel, another race of rainbows follows a quite different path. Upon reaching about seven inches in length, these fish migrate downstream some 200 miles to the Pacific Ocean, feed voraciously on the bounty of the ocean for one or two full years, and then return to spawn as a six to 12 pound, chrome-bright steelhead trout.

A TROUT'S LIFE CYCLE

The following is a general survey of the life cycle of a typical wild trout, stressing the similarities between the three species.

All true trout spawn in cold, moving water. Brook "trout," though similar in appearance and behavior to trout, are actually a member of the char genus, and can spawn in either still or moving water.

Trout are cold-blooded vertebrae. They thrive in water of 45-60 degrees Fahrenheit. As water temperature exceeds 60 degrees, trout struggle to get enough oxygen. As cold-blooded organisms, their metabolism and body temperature increase and decrease to match water temperature. Thus when food is most abundant during the summer their activity level is highest. Recognition of this fundamental fact puts to rest the old nonsense that in early spring fishing will be great because the fish are hungry from a winter with little food.

Eggs Sheltering in the Redd

Trout begin life as eggs incubating in the gravel of their natal stream. The size and quality of the spawning gravel are critical to trout egg survival. Gravel needs to be at least 4/10 inch in diameter to allow for spaces between the gravel sufficient to allow for circulation of water and with it much needed dissolved oxygen.

Cold, clean water is needed to nurture trout. If silt is present in the water it may prevent the eggs from receiving oxygen and thus kill them.

When water temperature is 45 degrees, rainbow trout eggs take about 48 days to incubate and hatch; brown trout eggs in this water would take about 64 days. As water temperatures increase these periods decrease; as temperatures decrease the incubation periods increase.

Alevin

When the eggs hatch, one-inch long "alevin" result. The large pendulous sac hanging below the main fish contains nutrient, a little lunch box if you will, and during this period the alevin absorbs these nutrients.

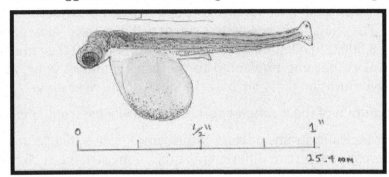

Alevin

Swim-up

The alevin remain in the gravel for a period lasting from two weeks to four months, absorbing the nutrients in the egg sac and dissolved oxygen from the circulating water. As they sense that the nutrients within the egg sac are being consumed, they begin to crawl their way up through the gravel, a process termed "swim-up," and become free-swimming *fry*, about one inch long, complete fish with tiny eyes, mouth, and tails. They now will need to forage for themselves.

Swim-up

They enter a world bereft of maternal nurture and steeped in competition for survival. The human concepts of mercy and charity have no place in this world. All trout are cannibals; therefore, they are preyed upon by their older siblings as well as other fish.

They instinctively seek shelter behind or aside large rocks, within aquatic vegetation, and, by hook or crook, fend for their lives.

Free-swimming fry

Fry Growth and Development

Out of 1,000 eggs laid by a spawning female in the spring, by end of summer perhaps 10-30 fry will still be alive. Those fortunate few now feed on aquatic insects and grow, all the while nervously looking over their shoulders for those who would make a meal of them.

Potential Out-migration as Smolts

As mentioned above, some races of trout are genetically programmed to out-migrate to a lake or to salt water. This out-migration, termed *smoltification*, usually occurs during the spring, when most streams are flowing at their greatest volume.

Smoltification occurs when the juvenile trout reach a certain stage of growth, typically about seven inches in length. Their age when they reach this size is typically one to three years, and is dependent on the availability of food in their natal stream.

The juvenile fish begin to show a silver coloration on their sides, and internal hormonal changes allow them to adjust to salt water.

Adults

The surviving trout continue to feed on available organisms. For the fresh water trout: aquatic and terrestrial insects, small fish of all sorts, and freshwater crustaceans. For the ocean dwellers: shrimp, herring, and small salmon. Their growth is directly related to the abundance of food and varies tremendously between streams, lakes and the ocean.

Generally speaking, lakes offer more food than streams, and the ocean has more food than lakes. That the ocean's bounty is so great compared to a freshwater stream can be appreciated by the fact that a typical pre-migrant steelhead might spend two years in a freshwater stream attaining a length of six or seven inches, then spend two years in the salt water and grow into an enormous 26 to 28-inch fish.

Alkaline water is usually more productive than acidic water, either in a lake or in a stream.

A trout's growth, whether it be in a stream, a lake or the ocean, takes place during the warm seasons. Trout may actually lose weight over the winter.

The life story of an individual fish can be determined by studying a scale sample. Like reading the rings on a tree cross section, the scales display rings caused by winter versus summer growth and spawning.

Sexual Maturity and Spawning

The age at which trout reach sexual maturity varies greatly based on the abundance or sparseness of available food and on their specific life history strategy. Resident trout require at least two or three years to mature; Anadromous trout usually require one to four years as pre-migrants followed by an additional one to three years in the saltwater.

Anadromous trout, driven by spawning urges, will migrate back to the natal stream; resident trout may migrate as little as a few hundred yards. Both, upon arrival at the natal stream, will seek suitable spawning gravel and mating partners.

Both sexes undergo physical changes in preparation for spawning or as a byproduct of sexual maturity. Their coloration becomes vivid. The red stripe on rainbows is enlarged. The cutthroat's namesake slashes below the jaw turn vivid red. Males often develop a "kype," a pronounced hook on the extreme front of the lower jaw. They also grow extra teeth, and the ridge from the head to the dorsal fin enlarges.

Using her tail, the adult spawning female digs an oval-shaped depression into the gravel to create a nest of sorts, termed a "redd." The quantity of eggs an adult female trout carries is in direct relationship to its size: a one-pound trout may carry about 1,000 eggs; a 12-pound steelhead perhaps 10,000.

Redd-building attracts nearby spawning males who compete to mate with as many females as possible. The successful male positions himself alongside the female. When the redd is complete to their satisfaction, both will begin quivering and simultaneously expel eggs and milt into the gravel. The female will immediately move upstream of the redd and dig into the gravel with her tail, covering the eggs and filling the depression. This second digging may become a second redd if the first extrusion of eggs was incomplete.

By wise tradition anglers have considered spawning adults to be off limits to angling. The reasons are compelling: the fish are in poor condition and do not fight well; the potential for snagging, intentional or otherwise, is high; they are not actively feeding; and fishing regulations typically work to prohibit it.

Mended Spawners

The rigors of spawning leave a trout dark, thin, and weak. The males in particular are weakened though both sexes are affected. Unlike Pacific salmon, all of whom die after spawning once, spawning trout can survive, "mend," and live to spawn multiple times in future years. However many do die from the rigors of spawning and few actually spawn a second time.

For years fish biologists have observed that once a trout has reached sexual maturity, its growth slows and may plateau. For this reason, biologists like to find ways to breed sterile hatchery trout whose growth would continue throughout their lives, therefore creating trophy specimens. The latest effort in this direction is called a *triploid trout*, and is based on a naturally occurring anomaly in which the individual has three sets of chromosomes rather than two. A triploid trout, whether naturally occurring or produced in a hatchery, is sterile but functions normally in all other respects. Its growth continues throughout its life. Another purpose of triploid trout stocking is to avoid hybridization with existing native trout.

The "True" Trouts

While many names are given to trout throughout the world, biologists only recognize three species or "true" trouts: rainbow, cutthroat, and brown. The many local and regional names for trout are in large part due to the trout's chameleon-like ability to change its coloration to blend in with its varied environment, ranging from the open ocean to tiny mountain streams to peat-colored beaver ponds.

Basic Trout Anatomy

Differentiating between trout and other fish and between the trout species is an essential skill for all anglers. Catching and observing fish in the wild can be augmented between fishing trips by reviewing these pages and other sources and thus becoming aware of the identifying features.

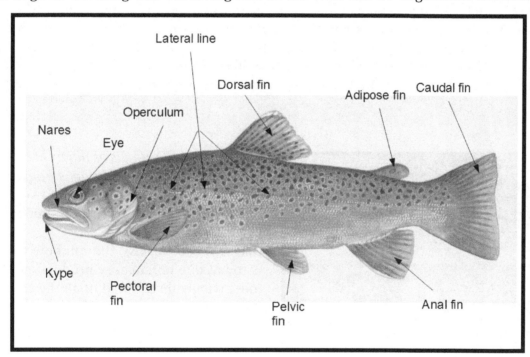

Painting courtesy of U.S. Fish and Wildlife Service; labels by author.

The Nervous System

A brief review of a trout's nervous system should prove instructive to anyone interested in fishing. The trout's nervous system includes the following:

Eyes. Make no mistake about it–trout have excellent vision. They have no eyelids, which means that they will want to avoid bright light. Rivers flowing north (in the Northern Hemisphere) cause the current-holding trout to face directly into the sun's rays for much of the day. They won't be inclined to look upwards and rise to a surface fly until the sun goes off the water.

Nares (nostrils). The two nostrils are located above the eyes on each side, and include front and rear openings that allow water to constantly flow through the olfactory sac where it is smelled. As noted above the trout's ability to sense changes in water chemicals via the olfactory process is simply mind-boggling.

Lateral Line. Senses changes in water pressure and reverberations in the water caused by an angler's stumbling over stones, banging a wading staff on the river floor, or throwing an anchor into a lake.

Inner Ear. Works in conjunction with the lateral line to sense "noises" in the water.

Brain. A trout's brain is a fraction of the size, in relation to its overall body, of that of a human. But consider further the composition of the trout's brain compared to the human: There is no equivalent to the cerebrum, and the optic and olfactory lobes are huge.

Think like a fish????

The above description of the trout's brain above should demonstrate the silliness of the old advice "think like a fish." If you were to actually think like a fish, you would not be capable of even unlocking the trunk of your car, let alone assembling your fly rod and walking to the stream. The trout simply has no logic processing ability.

Better advice comes from my old Boy Scout Handbook back in 1963. The wonderful old Scout handbooks were packed with practical lore on camping and nature. One outdoor skill taught in the manual was termed "stalking." Today you would rightly get arrested for this activity, but in 1963 it meant sneaking up on a deer or rabbit or whatever wildlife you encountered. The drawings in the old Scout manual showed a large cat (probably a cougar) stalking a rabbit eating grass. When the rabbit took a bite of the plant and chewed, the cougar would advance a step. When the rabbit stopped and looked around in between bites, the cougar froze and waited. That's the sort of skills we need to learn.

The Rainbow Trout

Rainbow trout. Photo by U.S. Fish and Wildlife Service.

Rainbow trout fishing is as different from brook fishing as prizefighting is from boxing.

–Ernest Hemingway

Oncorhynchus mykiss, the rainbow trout, is today, due to hatchery production, the most widely distributed of all the trouts. Its original range extended along the Pacific Rim from Mexico, north to Alaska, across the Aleutian chain and across the Kamchatka Peninsula in Russia. Biologists prefer rainbow over cutthroat or brown for hatchery culture because of its hardiness in the face of hatchery-bred diseases.

Rainbows can be identified by their namesake pink band running the full length of the lateral line and splashed on the gill covers. The back is a dark blue to olive green turning silvery below towards the belly. The back, sides, head, and fins are covered by small black spots.

Their coloration varies greatly depending on the local aquatic environment. Rainbows in the ocean or lake, or having recently returned, may be so silver that the lateral stripe is nearly invisible.

Rainbows spawn in the spring, but this varies greatly between watersheds and races and may occur any time between January and June.

Rainbows tend to be strongly migratory, searching out any lake or the salt water that affords access out and then back again to spawn. Their beauty, acrobatic fighting, and willingness to hit a fly have endeared them to anglers for generations.

Migratory strains that have clear access to the ocean leave their natal stream at two to four years of age and spend one, two, or more years in the salt water. Here they gorge on the bounty of the ocean: other fish, squid, and amphipods. They return to their natal streams to spawn as the celebrated steelhead trout, weighing from five to twenty or more pounds upon their return. Rainbows migrating to an accessible lake may potentially return to the river for feeding runs in addition to an annual spawning run of sexually mature fish.

The late September sun was fast setting as I cast across the Deschutes River. I had waded mid-thigh into the cool, gentle flow. The water to which I cast seemed picture-perfect steelhead water: an even flow with a choppy surface, about four or five feet deep, flowing along at a fast walk pace. My nine-foot, seven-weight rod, matched with a floating line, cast and mended nicely across the even current. At the business end, a #4 Muddler Minnow. I've learned to put faith in this fly.

And faith you must have to catch a steelhead.

This was my third day-trip to the Deschutes that season, and I had yet to have a steelhead strike. On this day, I had been casting about five hours without a single take. Steelhead, the fish of a thousand casts. It was that time in the day that the steelheader chases doubts circling in out of consciousness. Maybe this drift had been worked too hard by other anglers; maybe I have the wrong fly; or, perhaps, the steelheader's chronic doubt, the fish are laying out there just a few yards beyond the reach of my 60-foot casts.

Perhaps an hour remained before the legal fishing deadline. I would fish out the day, but I knew that wasn't good enough, just to fish until the deadline. The steelheader needs to fish each cast like he or she expects a strike on that very cast.

The fly slowly worked its way down and across the current. The sun was directly above the fly line, and I squinted hard to keep the fly line in my vision. The fish struck at the end of the drift, the fly directly downriver from me. I felt a hard pull and then an authoritative run across the stream. I carefully worked downstream over the grapefruit-sized rock bottom. This fish was not a jumper but made up for it in strong runs, taking me far into the fly line backing before I could turn him. After the fish had made several such runs, I was still working downstream, now looking for a suitable spot to beach the fish. The riverbank was lined by trees and brush, but I saw a gap in the vegetation through which I could wade to shore and beach the fish.

Now I could feel the head of the fish coming out of the water and he was ready to beach. I slid the fish into shallow water and admired its beauty. Thirty inches in length, still silver on its flanks with a slender pink stripe. Wild or hatchery? The Deschutes hosts both. Adipose and pelvic fines all intact, the dorsal fin straight and true. A wild steelhead. I removed the barbless hook, cradled the fish, pointed him upstream and watched him swim away, into the depths of the river.

Painting courtesy of U.S. Fish and Wildlife Service.

The cutthroat trout, *Oncorhynchus clarkii*, originally ranged throughout much of the western United States and Canada, from Southeast Alaska to the Eel River in California, from the Pacific Ocean to the eastern slope of the Rocky Mountains, as far east as South Platte River in Colorado and the Rio Grande in New Mexico.

The cutthroat has many regional variants, some of which have been formally identified as subspecies. Sadly, many of these have been lost due to a litany of environmental degradations.

Streamside identification can be determined by its namesake crimson slashes found just below the jaw. However, sea-run fish fresh from the salt water may not display these marks or they may be nearly indistinct. The first few sea-run cutthroats I caught I refused to believe were cutthroat due to the lack of the red "cutthroat" markings; I insisted that they were small steelhead.

The coastal cutthroat, *Oncorhynchus clarkii clarkii*, is a recognized subspecies. It inhabits the western portion of the cutthroat range. The cutthroat can be migratory, but is not as strongly migratory as the rainbow. In waters open to salt water it will migrate downstream to the estuaries and bays, sometimes migrating into the ocean but only for short periods and generally staying close to the river mouth. Most fish return each winter to their natal stream.

In the Pacific Northwest, these sea-run cutthroats are prized as a game fish of the highest order. They are pursued by anglers tossing wet flies, dry flies, spinners, and bait. Unfortunately, destructive logging practices, dams, over-fishing, and indiscriminate development have taken their toll, and today in many streams only remnant runs remain as a sad reminder of their former glory.

When I moved to Vancouver, Washington, in 1977, sea-run cutthroat numbers were sufficient to sustain a popular, late-summer "plunking" fishery on the tidewater stretches of streams such as the Lewis and Kalama. Families gathered along the beaches, kids and old folks, barbeques smoking and radios playing, spin rods propped up in holders. Waiting for the "harvest trout" to strike a glob of night crawlers down near the bottom of the slow-moving tidewater. Go there now in August and no one is there.

But there are still a few fish around, enough to keep us interested and hopeful. Today catch and release and restricted gear regulations are in place on many of these same streams in an effort to bring back these beautiful fish. In the state of Washington, due to budget cuts, sea-run cutthroat hatchery programs have been eliminated on most streams. The approach now is to bring back the wild fish.

Labor Day weekend found me on the banks of the Nehalem River at the upper limit of tidewater. Here the incoming high tide mix with the "sweet" or freshwater currents flowing to the ocean. Sea-run cutthroat trout are the gypsies of the salmonids, moving in seemingly random fashion throughout the bays and tidal stretches of rivers, eventually committing themselves to the freshwater river sometime between August and December in preparation for spawning later in the winter or early spring.

Often the sea-runs will enter the river proper on a high tide, then recede back to the bay or ocean with the ebb tide. But it is not that straightforward. Anglers study and look for patterns; sometimes the fish cooperate, often they don't.

Directly above tidewater, I worked a streamer pattern through several runs without result. The sun was hot, and I retreated to shade. A rag-tag quartet of ten-year-olds, with that innocent exuberance of boyhood, played in the river: rooting in the mud for bugs, splashing each other, collecting stones, taking advantage of the final days of summer. Soon they found a spot on the river where the gentle current allowed them to float downstream for 10 or 15 yards ending in a slow pool where they could wade out, hike up to the head of the current, and float down again. I watched them from the shade; time seemed to stand still.

Later the kids went home to supper, and the cooling air and lengthening shadows called me back to the river. The tide had flowed in, and I worked a Spruce fly down and across the slow current that dumped into a deep tidewater pool. The fly swung around in the soft current and hung on the edge of the deep pool, and then slowly I retrieved the fly. The first fish grabbed the fly just after my cast hit the water and pulled hard, jumped once, and dove down into the pool. It was a good fish and well hooked. He pulled hard but did not jump again. As he tired I brought him to hand and admired the beauty of a strong, wild fish, fresh from the ocean: thirteen inches in length, strong and plump from feeding in the bay and ocean; tiny x-shaped spots against a silver background; the full dorsal fin like a sailboat's mainsail proudly announced its wild origins. Below the jaw, a very faint orange slash. I admired him briefly then slid him back into the pool.

No more than ten minutes later as I was beginning my retrieve, a strong pull and another good sea-run, perhaps the twin of the first. After a good fight, he too was released.

The Brown Trout

Brown trout. Painting by U.S. Fish and Wildlife Service.

The brown trout, *Salmo trutta*, is the native trout of the British Isles, the birthplace of fly fishing. Originally flourishing throughout Europe, it has been out-planted over much of the United States as well as to Argentina and New Zealand.

The brown trout's general appearance is large, dark spots over a brown background. Brown trout can thrive in marginally warmer water than rainbow or cutthroat, making them attractive to hatchery biologists for out-planting in lowland lakes where summer temperatures become dangerously warm.

Anglers have forever compared various game species in terms of prized qualities, and in this game the brown trout is often touted as the more difficult trout to catch, and the rainbow is often revered as the strongest, wildest fighter. Such generalizations are dangerous, but there must be some truth to these adages, realizing that the condition of the trout and the environment in which it resides play an important role as well.

Unlike rainbow and cutthroat trout, browns typically spawn during the fall. There exist anadromous races, called "sea-trout" in the British Isles. Sea-trout spend several years in the ocean and return to spawn as bright-silver trophies ranging from three to eight or more pounds.

One spring when I was learning to fly fish, I fished for bluegills and crappie in Lacamas Lake near my home. I would follow the shoreline in my car-top boat and cast to schools of bluegills. That spring I learned how to cast and learned I could actually catch fish on a fly. One evening I called it quits, loaded the car-top into my truck, then wandered back to the lake shore to relax and enjoy the lake for a few minutes before the drive home. I spotted a fly fisher out in the lake casting to rising fish that did not look like the bluegills I had caught all afternoon. Fish were rising in a group and he was catching them with some regularity.

I waited until he took a break and talked to him. They were brown trout, and he showed me the fly: a #14 nymph with a white head, charcoal-colored body, and a silver ribbing. A typical chironomid imitation. He said he cast to where he saw rises and slowly stripped in the fly, "just to keep in contact with the fly."

On my next outing to the lake I stayed through the evening and was equipped with a supply of the chironomid flies. Following his technique, I caught several brown trout. They were hatchery fish, only about ten or eleven inches long, but still attractive and gave a decent fight. I returned on other evenings that spring and continued my learning. These were among the first trout I had ever caught on the fly. In the subsequent years I would catch browns in other lakes throughout the Pacific Northwest, but have not yet fished for them in rivers, nor for sea-run browns. Lots to keep me busy over whatever remaining years I am granted.

Wild Trout Needs

- Cold, clean, well-oxygenated water. At temperatures above 60 degrees Fahrenheit dissolved oxygen declines and fish may be stressed.

- Protection from predators. Rocks, logs, rapids, plant life all can provide hiding places from predators.

- Food. Sufficient aquatic insects, small fish, or terrestrial insects.

- Spawning gravel. Trout require clean gravel with cold, clear water flowing over and through it. Siltation can kill trout eggs.

Hatchery Trout

Hatchery production of trout began at least 80 years ago, and is utilized by most states' fisheries departments. An important debate has been waged for decades in the fly fishing community concerning hatcheries versus wild fish. This debate is outside of the scope of this book, but I want to introduce those readers unfamiliar with the issues to a few basic concepts.

Hatchery production can have one or more goals; therefore each hatchery program must be understood and evaluated apart from other programs. To speak of "hatcheries" in a general sense is misleading and unproductive.

Here are some of the diverse purposes of hatchery programs:

- To introduce trout into lakes that lack inlet streams for spawning but otherwise provide acceptable and in some cases exceptional trout habitation. Examples of these applications are most of the Kamloops lakes in British Columbia and the seep lakes in Eastern Washington.

- To meet legal requirements for mitigation for loss of spawning habitat caused by hydroelectric power dams.

- To supplement natural trout or salmon production to meet intense fishing pressure.

Hatchery Trout Life Cycle

A hatchery trout program begins with the selection of the broodstock to be used. All hatchery fish begin with wild fish and without them there would be no hatchery fish. Broodstock are adult fish that are artificially stripped of their eggs and milt which are then artificially spawned to produce trout. The choice of broodstock is critical to the results of the hatchery program. In the past too often non-native stocks were utilized with insufficient consideration for the preservation of unique gene pools.

Fertilized eggs are grown in incubators which correspond to the redds of naturally spawning fish. Upon hatching, the fry are grown in large cement tanks and fed commercial food.

The size at which the trout are released into the wild is an important variable. Some programs, derisively called "put and take," release "catchable" trout into waters, often the opening day of fishing season. Other programs release fry rather than catchables, thus allowing natural selection to have at least some effect, and allowing the fish to reside in the natural environment for an extended period, perhaps a year, before being subject to harvest.

Lately there have been efforts in many states to reform hatchery programs in the light of current scientific understanding. Hatcheries now, more than in the past, stress preserving and building up wild trout gene pools. We hope.

Distinguishing Wild from Hatchery Trout

A critical skill for all anglers is to distinguish wild trout from their hatchery brethren, at the point of capture, in order to make the right decision concerning release vs kill. ***All wild trout should be released.***

The fins tell the story:

- Adipose Fin. Currently (in 2018), the fisheries departments in the states of Washington, Oregon, California, and Idaho all clip the adipose fins of hatchery steelhead and salmon, and in some cases trout. State law in each of these states define wild steelhead and salmon by the presence of the adipose fin, and legal protection of these fish is in force for all fish with an intact adipose fin. Be sure to read your state regs book carefully and understand how this works. It may change in the future, so be sure to know the up to date rules.

- Dorsal Fin. Confined to pens with thousands of siblings, in tight proximity not found in the wild, the hatchery fingerlings nip at each other's dorsal fins. This behavior is so widespread that the adult hatchery fish invariably displays a jagged dorsal fin that contrasts with the full, natural rays of the wild trout's fin.

- Pelvic Fins. As above, hatchery operations may clip one of these fins for identification purposes. Be sure to carefully read your state's fishing regulations to become aware of what clippings may be currently in force, and in which streams.

10. Other Freshwater Gamefish of the Pacific Northwest

Trout are no doubt the most popular fly rod quarry, and this book focuses on techniques for catching them. This chapter discusses other freshwater gamefish of the Pacific Northwest that I've enjoyed fishing for.

.

Panfish, Family Centrarchidae

Panfish is a rather unscientific but serviceable term for "pan-size" warm-water, spiny-ray fish, such as bluegill, white crappie, black crappie, banded sunfish, largemouth bass, and dozens of other members of the Centrarchidae family. All of them display a dorsal fin that includes a forward portion consisting of from seven to 11 razor-sharp rays, followed by a rear section with softer rays more like a trout. These forward-spiny-rays can leave nasty cuts on your hands. I learned to reach down while the fish is still in the water, grab the barbless fly, and free it with a sharp yank without touching the fish.

Bluegill. Photo courtesy of Mike Cline.

All panfish are warm-water fish, thriving in water far too warm for trout. Also unlike trout, they spawn in still water. These two characteristics allow panfish to flourish in low-elevation ponds and lakes, waters marginal for trout. You probably have several such ponds in your vicinity and they probably host panfish.

So, don't limit your casting practice to a lawn. Locate a couple of warm-water ponds that have panfish, and get out there and have fun! I learned to cast and

Largemouth Bass

caught my first fish on a fly in such a pond some 40 years ago. A five or six-weight rod recommended in Chapter 6, matched with a floating line will work just fine. If you have a lighter rod, a three or four-weight, all the better. Panfish are not picky as regards to flies. I just tie on a barbless #12 or #14 dark nymph, maybe a Pheasant Tail or a Hair's Ear. I row around the shoreline, casting towards shore, or logs, or lily pads. Lots of fun and excellent casting practice at the same time.

Char, Genus *Salvelinus*

The members of the *Salvelinus* genus are closely related to trout both in scientific taxonomy and in the minds and hearts of anglers. Brook trout, arctic char, Dolly Varden, and bull trout are well known members.

A key difference between trout and char is spawning behavior. Trout spawn only in moving water, but many char species can spawn in either moving or still water.

Brook trout were originally native to eastern North America in the United States and Canada. Today they have been exported to waters throughout the globe. Since they are prolific spawners, in many lakes and rivers individual brook trout remain small. With more mouths to feed and a fixed amount of food, they adapt, but often sexually mature adults average no more than eight or nine inches in length.

Dolly Varden thrive in Alaska and British Columbia, where they share watersheds with their larger and more glamorous relatives, the Pacific salmons. The fish's feminine nickname refers to the Charles Dickens character *Miss Dolly Varden*, whose flamboyant, pink-spotted dress came to mind when some early anglers admired the brightly-spotted fish. Though typically a stream resident, it can also migrate to sea, returning stronger and larger than its stay-at- home cousins.

Sea-run Dolly Varden. Photo courtesy of M. Martinz.

The **bull trout** was first recognized as a species in 1980; prior to then it was generally lumped in with Dolly Varden. Since 1998 the bull trout has been listed as *threatened* under the Endangered Species Act throughout its range. Bull trout require cold, clear water, averaging 55 degrees, even colder than the trouts.

Mountain Whitefish, *Prosopium williamsoni*

Some folks consider the whitefish a nuisance and deny its status as a gamefish. I disagree. Whitefish will take a wet fly or nymph and fight well though refraining from the aerial acrobatics of the rainbow trout. They generally feed on or near the bottom of a river, thus a deep-sunk nymph can be effective. In some western rivers the whitefish provides a substantial winter fishery.

The Pacific Salmons, Genus Oncorhynchus

Collectively, the six species of Pacific salmon comprise one of the most bountiful natural resources in the world. From Japan on the eastern Pacific, north to Alaska, then south along the western Pacific shoreline as far south as Los Angeles, rivers great and small host (or did host) staggering numbers of seagoing salmon. Five of the six Pacific salmon species thrive in the Pacific Northwest; the diminutive cherry salmon lives only on the Asian side of the Pacific Ocean. Adults return to bays and estuaries after one to six years of gorging themselves on the ocean's bounty. Driven by spawning urges, some reaching fifty pounds or more, they enter the rivers each fall.

Salmon jump the falls. Photo courtesy of U.S. Fish and Wildlife Service

Angling for Pacific salmon attracts thousands who head to the bays and rivers in boats or line the banks as the fish return to fresh water. But the numbers of fly anglers amongst these hordes seem small. Fly fishing for Pacific salmon has not developed the following one would expect, given the popularity of fly fishing along the entire length of the West Coast and the fish's obviously attractive features. A major reason for this lack of interest is related to the cold, hard facts of the salmon's life cycle: As they sexually mature, their flesh deteriorates markedly, culminating with their death. After completing their one and only spawning season, all Pacific salmon die. As they enter fresh water their decline has already begun. After a few weeks in fresh water, salmon have transformed from beautiful, strong fish into dark, dying ghosts. They ignore any fly put in front of them. Snagging, both intentional and unintentional, is rampant, since the fish soon move into shallow water to spawn where they can be easily spotted. All their energy is concentrated on spawning and they become oblivious to other stimuli.

In the bays and estuaries, the fish are still in fine condition and will hit bait or lure, but to get a fly to them in the expansive waters of a bay is difficult. Hence most angling effort is with lures or bait, and often from boats capable of navigating the sizable waters of a coastal bay.

But fly anglers have identified unique situations in which the fly can be effective on Pacific salmon. In the salt water of Puget Sound, fly anglers work the beaches casting to feeding pink and resident coho salmon still months from sexual maturity; on the Smith River in Northern California, anglers cast large flies with sinking, shooting heads to spring Chinook salmon, a run that enters streams in the spring but do not spawn until fall.

In my admittedly limited experience, the key for being successful with Pacific salmon is to avoid the angling hordes on the rivers in the fall, and instead find experienced anglers who will point you towards those promising combinations of times, places, techniques, and species.

11. A Trout's Diet

Learning about the foods that fish feed upon can not only increase your catch rate, but can deepen your appreciation and enjoyment of fly fishing. One can catch fish without knowledge of aquatic insects, emergence tables, and the like. But catching fish, per se, is not, or should not be, the be-all and end-all of fly fishing. To participate in and increase our appreciation of nature, to increase the enjoyment of each fish caught–these are reasons many of us turn to fly fishing.

But learning about aquatic insects can seem overwhelming not just to the beginner but to many experienced fly anglers; keep in mind that you can enjoy fishing and catch fish without an extensive knowledge of insects, and as you learn and advance in the sport your knowledge will build over time.

So don't be overwhelmed. Just fish, learn, and enjoy.

Aquatic Insects in General

Aquatic insects form a sizable share of a trout's freshwater diet. Very few insects live In salt water, and trout residing there must pursue other food, which they find in abundance. The life cycles of aquatic insects include distinct stages, and the advancement through each stage is termed *metamorphosis.* Insects are classified as having one of three life cycles:

- *Complete metamorphosis*–includes egg, larvae, pupa, and adult. Typified by the caddisfly and chironomid

- *Incomplete metamorphosis*–includes egg, nymph, and adult. Typified by the mayfly and the stonefly

- *No metamorphosis–few insects are in this category and they are not important to trout.*

Insects, like trout, have scientific, Latin names for each order, family, genus, and species, and also common names used by anglers. The common names are often locally derived nicknames and thus potentially confusing.

As has often been noted, very few trout can read or write Latin. Therefore I list the common names for insects, as well the scientific names to aid in referencing other works.

Each species of aquatic insect has its own internal clock that tells it to emerge when air and water temperatures reach certain conditions. Emergence, or more accurately "mass emergence," is synonymous with the anglers' term "hatch." During an emergence, it is likely that trout will concentrate on the hatching insects. For this reason, fly anglers study and target the hatches on their local streams and lakes. Since they vary greatly from region to region, I have not listed emergence tables in this book, but encourage the reader to obtain local knowledge about hatches, which can be obtained from fly shops, internet sites, your local newspaper outdoor column, other anglers, and, of course, your own observations.

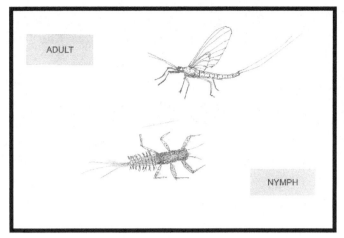

Typical mayfly adult and nymph.

Along with birds singing, rhododendrons and azaleas blooming, baseball players warming up for practice, an evening hatch of mayflies helps announce the arrival of spring. With their graceful, sail-shaped wings and long, tapered bodies, they have a well-established association with fly fishing. To read English authors from a century ago, one might conclude that fly fishing means fishing exclusively mayfly dry flies.

The Mayfly Life Cycle

1. Eggs. Mayflies begin life as eggs clinging to the bottom of a lake or river.

2. Nymphs. When the eggs hatch, *nymphs* result. Mayfly nymphs typically live for a year. Of the three stages of a mayfly's life, the nymph stage displays the most behavioral diversity. Each species of mayfly can be categorized as one of the following based on the behavior of the nymph:

-**Burrowers**. Live in lakes with soft muddy bottoms. The nymphs burrow into the mud and remain there until emergence, thus are not available to trout until that time. Examples: Hexagenia and Brown Drake.

-**Swimmers**. Unlike the other three kinds of mayfly nymphs, these streamlined little guys are active swimmers, darting back and forth between pillar and post. They thrive in both lakes and streams. Examples: Blue-winged Olives and *Callibaetis*.

-**Crawlers.** These rascals crawl slowly across the river or lake bottom; if dislodged, swim poorly and make a nice meal for a waiting trout. Usually found in streams. Examples: Pale Morning Dun and Green Drake.

-**Clingers.** Their flattened shape helps them cling to rocks in fast-moving streams. But when dislodged, their poor swimming ability causes them to bounce downstream and possibly into the feeding lanes of deep-holding trout. Examples: Western March Brown and Little Yellow May.

3. Nymphs Emerging. Driven by changing air and water temperatures and their own growth, the nymphs at some point "emerge," i.e., swim to the surface of the lake or stream, break out of their exoskeleton, break through the surface film, and float on the surface.

4. Adults Drying Wings. The adults must dry their wings before they can fly away. How long depends upon the air temperature, humidity and other factors.

5. Adults: Final Molting, Mating, and Depositing Eggs. The adults fly to nearby vegetation and make a final molting (shedding skin) preparatory to mating. Mating occurs in swarms above the water culminating with the eggs being deposited on the surface of the water to sink and attach themselves to underwater vegetation or rocks. The adult stage of mayflies lasts from as little as a few hours to two days. This ephemeral existence yields its Latin name: *Ephemeroptera*.

CADDISFLIES, ORDER TRICHOPTERA

Caddisfly illustration from "British Entomology" by James Francis Stephens, from Wiki Commons.

The first full-blown "hatch" I encountered, identified, and from which I actually caught some nice trout occurred many years ago on the White River in Central Oregon. Having heard of the wonderful fishing on the Deschutes River, I drove the 120 miles from my home to the river for a June day trip. I fished here and there, tried a multitude of flies, and found myself at sunset tired, hot, thirsty and fish-less.

Driving home, I remembered that just a few miles homeward, the highway crossed the White River, a major tributary of the Deschutes. So, when I reached the bridge, I did what any self-respecting fly fishing nut would do: I stopped the car, got out the fly rod, and headed for the stream.

I hiked a hundred yards or so through a sparse, dry pine forest, and met with a tiny side-channel to the main river no more than a yard wide. I tossed my fly onto a tiny tongue of current and immediately a small fish grabbed my #12 Hare's Ear Nymph. I brought him in quickly and examined him. At first I wasn't sure it was a trout: only eight inches long but incredibly plump, with a full, straight dorsal fin announcing its wild origins. For a guy who caught his first few trout from the relatively unproductive waters of Western Washington, this trout looked downright obese. I quickly released him and headed for the main river.

What I saw there astonished me. The water seemed to boil with good-sized trout rising, splashing everywhere to tan-colored caddisflies. Everywhere; every second or so one would break the surface. Some jumped right out of the water to grab adult caddis as they flew away from the river. The trout were all sizes from my little eight-inch friend to well over fifteen inches.

Not knowing for certain what fly to use, judging that the Hare's Ear looked about the right color and size, I began casting across and downstream, and in short order hooked and landed a nice, plump, twelve-inch trout. Over the next twenty minutes, I caught many more, missed many strikes, and hooked and lost others. I began to notice a huge trout on the far side of the river no more than 10 yards away consistently rising in the same spot about a yard below a large, overhanging branch. I cast to him time and time again but he ignored my offerings. By now the first few stars were out and it was time to drive home; I in a much better mood than before.

What specific species were the insects? I didn't know. But I knew they were caddis, and they were tan colored, just like the Hare's Ear Nymph fly I was fishing.

There are over 10,000 species of caddisflies, but you don't need to learn what each is. Caddisflies come in many different sizes and shades of color but all have the same basic shape and life cycle. Caddis, in England called "sedge," experience a *complete metamorphosis*, meaning they experience separate stages of larva and pupa, in place of the mayflies' single nymph stage.

Caddis typically inhabit moving water, but occasionally are found in lakes.

The caddisfly life cycle

1. **Eggs:** The tiny eggs attach themselves to underwater vegetation and incubate for a period lasting from several days to a month at which time the newly hatched larvae begin feeding on their own.

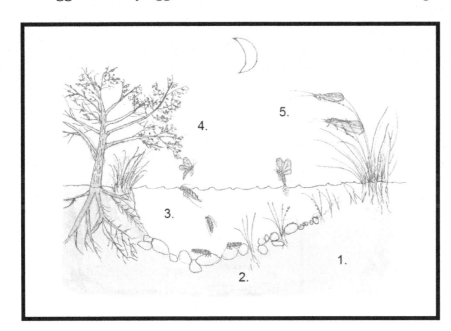

2. **Larvae** live on the bottoms of rivers and feed on minute plant life. Many are case-builders, coating themselves with stones and sticks. The popular nick-name of "periwinkles" applies to case-building caddis larvae. Other caddis do not build cases and are termed free-living.

3. **Pupae**: At a certain point in their development the larvae cover itself with a thin "cocoon" and then transforms itself into an adult. The wing pads develop. Pupation can take several weeks to over a month. When developed, the pupa migrates to the surface and breaks out into a fully formed adult. Some species, such as the huge October Caddis, instead of emerging in open water, swim to shore and crawl out onto rocks and from there fly to nearby vegetation.

4. **Adults:** The newly hatched adults waste little time on the water's surface, flying quickly to nearby vegetation. Unlike mayflies, they can live as adults for weeks or in some cases even months, returning periodically to the water to drink.

5. **Adults mating and egg-laying**: The adults mate on stream-side vegetation. Following mating, the females return to the stream, and either deposit eggs on the water's surface, or alternatively, swim underwater and deposit the eggs on the river bottom.

Important Points about Caddisflies

When caddisflies emerge, they quickly leave the water's surface without needing to dry their wings like mayflies. Therefore, trout often rise to the surface and take caddis while they are still pupae, rather than true adults. The caddis pupae must break through the water's surface film, and at this point they are highly vulnerable to trout.

All caddisflies have the same basic shape. The resting adults fold their wings in an inverted "V," or often described as looking like a long, skinny pup-tent.

Some biologists believe that caddisflies thrive better in poorer quality water than do mayflies or stoneflies.

Caddisflies vary greatly in size; most adults targeted by anglers range from 1/10 inch to 1 1/4 inches in length.

When trout feed near or on the surface for caddisflies, they often make "splashy" rises, sometimes jumping clear of the water.

STONEFLIES, ORDER PLECOPTERA

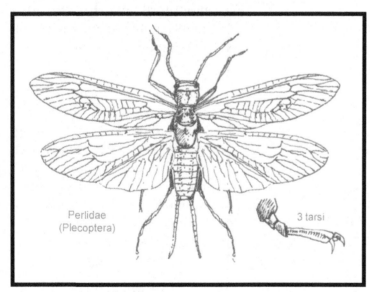

Stonefly, Plecoptera Perlidae, *drawing by Halvard Hatlen.*

About three years ago, my wife Teresa and I sat in a cafe in Beaune, France, enjoying a glass of wine. I often enjoy mentally time-traveling back in history at a given location. So I imagined: If we traveled back about 2.000 years, the Romans were strengthening their hold on the local residents and organizing the administration of the new province of Gaul. Go back about 200,000 years, and the Neanderthals walked upright, made tools, and buried their dead. Go back about 10,000,000 years, and the *Salmo* ancestors of the brown trout were swimming in nearby rivers. But you would need to go back about 260,000,000 years to see the first stoneflies crawling out of a river and flying away.

These primitive creatures go through a life cycle similar to mayflies, including the nymph and adult phases.

Typical stonefly life cycle

1.Eggs. The tiny eggs attach themselves to vegetation and incubate for a period ranging from a couple of days to several months.

2.Nymphs. All stonefly nymphs cling to the bottom of rocks and feed on both vegetation and other organisms. Unlike mayflies, stonefly nymphs have a gestation period of from one to three years. Thus, developing nymphs can be found in the water during any month of the year. That, plus their often-prodigious size, makes stonefly nymphs an important food source for trout and an opportunity for the nymph fisherman.

3. **Nymphs Emerge**. Unlike mayflies, stoneflies emerge by crawling towards shore onto exposed rocks or vegetation, then emerging from their exoskeleton and flying to nearby vegetation. Left littered on the rocks after an emergence are the thin "shucks" or exoskeletons.

4. **Adults**. The adults mate within a week of emergence. Mating takes place on streamside vegetation. Stonefly adults, unlike mayfly adults, are capable of eating. After mating, females of most species deposit the eggs by flying over the water and releasing eggs each time her abdomen touches the water. Being weak flyers, stoneflies are highly vulnerable at this stage. A few species of stoneflies deposit eggs by the females crawling under water and depositing the eggs directly on the bottom of the river.

Two species of stoneflies are celebrated by fly fishers throughout the west: the Golden Stone (*Acroneuria californica*) and the Giant Salmon Fly (*Pteronarcys californica*). Both are huge insects–the adults are as large as small birds (well, very small birds). Nearly two inches long, flopping helplessly on the water surface on a bright, late-spring day, Salmon Flies and Golden Stones can attract the largest trout to the banquet table (as well as hordes of anglers), on Pacific Northwest streams such as the Deschutes and the South Fork Boise.

Stoneflies are sensitive to declining water quality, and could be considered the insect counterpart to the cutthroat trout as the "canary in the mine."

During the early phase of the "hatch," the fully-developed nymphs migrate toward shore. Trout wait near the shore for individual nymphs to lose their grip on the bottom and tumble downstream.

Since they do not emerge through the surface film of the water like mayflies, don't expect a "hatch" on the surface of the water to occur. Look for the adults in the stream-side vegetation and cast close to shore near overhanging vegetation. Remember that the adults are weak fliers, thus when the wind kicks up some may be blown helpless onto the surface of the water.

CHIRONOMIDS, FAMILY CHIRONOMIDAE

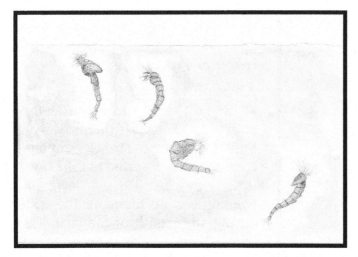

Chironomid pupa rising to the surface.

Chironomids, sometimes called "midges," are found in virtually every body of water, but they seem to be more important to fly anglers in lakes, at least in the Pacific Northwest. They progress through a complete metamorphosis: egg, larvae, pupa, and adult.

Chironomids may emerge during any month of the year. They vary greatly in size, from .04 of an inch to ½ inch in length. They are often very small, and in the 1930s, tiny, six-foot bamboo "midge rods" were developed for fishing the tiny hatches. But there are also sizable chironomids hatching and drawing good-sized trout to feed.

Chironomid larvae are small, tubular-shaped insects, rather nondescript in appearance. The larval stage lasts from about one month to about one year, then the critters enter the pupal stage, which lasts a few weeks. The pupae migrate towards the surface until they reach the surface film. Breaking through the film can take some time, and the insect is highly vulnerable at that point. Upon breaking through the film the adult quickly flies away. Mating occurs either on foliage or in the air, followed by the female's ovipositing the eggs on underwater foliage.

Most chironomid fishing targets the pupal stage. The larvae hide amongst the bottom foliage; the adults quickly leave the water's surface leaving little time for the trout to capture them.

DAMSELFLIES AND DRAGONFLIES, ORDER ODONATA

If you thought Odonata was a small city in southern Ukraine, then you are about where I was five or six years ago.

Walking along a pond or lake on a warm summer day you have probably often seen these large, dramatic insects flying and hovering about. Adult damselflies and dragonflies are the premier aviators of the insect world. Unlike stoneflies and many caddisflies, they are strong, confident fliers. The dragonfly in particular can fly up to thirty-five miles per hour, then stop suddenly and hover like an attack helicopter.

Odonata undergo an incomplete metamorphosis: egg, nymph, then adult.

The nymphs experience a one to five-year gestation period, thus like stoneflies, there are some of them around in different sizes all year long. And like stonefly nymphs, the mature nymphs crawl out onto rocks or others solid structures to molt and become adults. Thus, the emerger opportunity for fish, and anglers, doesn't happen.

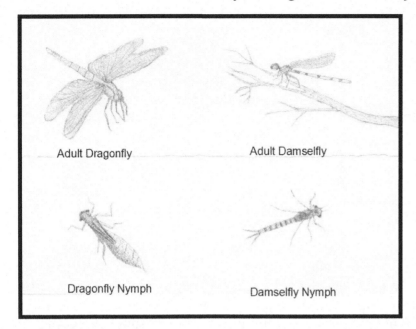

Adult Dragonfly

Adult Damselfly

Dragonfly Nymph

Damselfly Nymph

Unlike mayflies, Odonata lead a substantial adult life. For about two weeks prior to mating they feed on other insects, and each male establishes his own territory for mating and begins courting females. Mating occurs on streamside vegetation and egg-laying by females follows. Many adults die due to the rigors of mating, but some live for an additional period of several weeks.

In both the nymph and adult stages, dragonflies can be differentiated from damselflies by the former's stockier body. In the case of adults, the dragonfly at rest holds its wings outstretched at right angles to the body, while the damselfly holds hers parallel to the body and pointing somewhat upright.

The bread-and butter action for both the fish and the angler is the nymph stage. Well known flies, such as the Carey Special, imitate the damselfly nymph. Anglers over the years have toyed with the idea of imitating the substantial adult stage. In the 1930s, Canadian angler Bill Nation developed a fly he called Nation's Red to imitate mating dragonflies.

In the Pacific Northwest, most damselfly and dragonfly action is in lakes.

TERRESTRIALS

Land-based insects, termed terrestrials by anglers, often unwittingly find themselves flailing helplessly on the water's surface. Ants, beetles, bumblebees, flying termites, and grasshoppers are among the common terrestrial insects of interest to the trout, and therefore to the angler. A sudden gust of wind and the shaking of stream-side vegetation by humans or other critters are typical causes of their unhappy flight into the drink.

On lakes and larger rivers, the edges are the obvious place for terrestrials, since the wind will carry an insect only so far.

Since terrestrials land on the surface, most fishing for them is with dry flies.

BAITFISH

Trout eat all manner of small fish. Keep in mind that trout are cannibals. This runs counter to our sometimes anthropomorphic affection for trout, but in fact they are inveterate, unrepentant cannibals. Nature loves the species, but cares naught for the individual.

Many small fish other than salmonids can be found in both lakes and streams. Below are two examples from among many:

Sculpin, Family Cottidae, is found in most bodies of water and can be an important food source for trout. With its huge pectoral fins, bulging eyes, and pug-like face, it projects an evil, fantastic countenance. Bottom dwellers, their huge pectoral fins grip onto the substrate to help them maintain position against strong currents.

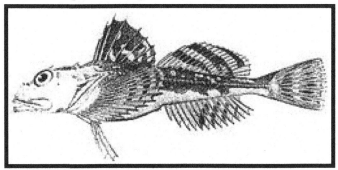

Longhorn Sculpin line art drawing, from the NEFSC historical photo archives.

Black-nosed Dace, Family Cyprindae. The Black-nosed Dace is a typical example of the Cyprindae family of fish, sometimes referred to as "minnows". They lack teeth and therefore feed on invertebrates and vegetation.

SALMON AND TROUT EGGS

On streams with substantial salmon runs, salmon eggs can be, in season, an important part of a trout's diet. The female salmon digs a nest, lays the eggs, and covers them with gravel, but the process is never 100 percent effective, therefore eggs leak out and tumble downstream. On many streams in Alaska, such as those in the Iliamna Lake region, huge rainbows, some exceeding ten pounds, migrate from the lakes up the streams to feast on salmon eggs. So I'm told.

SCUDS, ORDER AMPHIPODA

Scuds, often called "freshwater shrimp," are an important food source for trout. Scuds flourish in nutrient-rich alkaline waters as opposed to acidic lakes and streams. They thrive among the

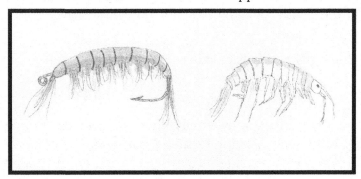

vegetation at the bottom of lakes and rivers. Scuds, being crustaceans, need calcium in the water to grow their exoskeleton. Scuds are typically ½ inch or less in length, but some, such as the Gammerus, can stretch to 1 inch. They don't "hatch"; their entire lives, birth, maturity, mating, and death, are spent underwater.

Scud and typical imitation.

"SELECTIVE" FEEDERS VERSUS "OPPORTUNISTIC" FEEDERS

Fly anglers often differentiate between trout feeding "selectively" versus trout feeding "opportunistically." Selective feeding refers to trout who, for a period of time, concentrate on one particular food source, be it nymph, pupa, adult insect, baitfish, salmon egg, or scud. When a hatch is going on, selective feeding on the emerging insects is a strong possibility. But there are times when a hatch is progressing and trout seem to ignore the hatching insects. They could be feeding on emerging nymphs or pupa or merely uninterested in the hatch.

Trout apparently decide to pursue or not pursue available food based on calories expended versus calories obtained, a "cost/benefit analysis." As discussed earlier, a trout's brain is incapable of logical thought, however they learn how many calories a given target will yield and figure out what it will take to capture that target. Thus trout will seemingly ignore floating mayfly adults and wait for, and attack, a "stillborn" mayfly, one that didn't, and won't, successfully hatch and fly away. The reason is obvious. When a trout rises to an adult mayfly drying his wings on the surface of the water, there is a good chance the mayfly will fly away before the trout reaches it. But with a stillborn adult there is no chance of it getting away.

Not very sporting of the trout, you say? It's a sport for us, it's survival for the trout.

When there is no hatch or compelling food source for the trout, they are inclined to feed opportunistically, for example they may hold near the bottom of the stream and wait for nymphs or other food to come drifting down the current to them. The cost/benefit principle is still at work: A trout will only move a certain distance for a piece of food. If it's bigger, he might move a little further to grab it. If he knows it will get away, he won't pursue it.

Matching the Hatch in Perspective

The term "matching the hatch" was either coined by or at least popularized by Ernest Schwiebert in the 1950s via his book of the same title. The title refers to an emphasis on fly selection that closely imitates whatever insect is currently emerging. Expected emergences are closely studied and flies are tied to exactly match the size, color, and shape of the expected hatch.

Criticism of this approach is that too great of an emphasis is placed on selecting the "correct" pattern to the exclusion of other success factors. Overdone matching the hatch reminds me of our grade-school janitor with his umpteen dozen keys on his huge keyring, trying each key in turn until the magic key finally unlocked the equipment closet so we boys could grab dodge-balls and race to the gym.

Before you go out and purchase 287 unique flies and prepare to do worthy battle, consider:

Fly selection is useless without proper fly *presentation*. Many expert anglers place the highest priority on presentation, with fly choice a secondary consideration. Fly fishing literature is filled with experts who limited themselves to a very few flies. Ed Van Put from the Catskills area uses only three patterns—the Adams, the Royal Wulff, and the Pheasant Tail Midge—and catches as many fish as those armed with several hundred flies.

> *At the other end of the scale, I met a gentleman fishing who claimed he carried "as many flies as many fly shops have in stock." He carried three rigged fly rods and a backpack full of flies. He opened it and showed me, and I would estimate that he was carrying at least 1,000 flies. And yes, the man could catch trout. I fished and talked to him on several outings and learned a great deal from him. He was knowledgeable not just about entomology, but also presentation, casting, watermanship, and more. Never got his name.*

Often (most of the time?) trout are NOT feeding selectively. Most of the time there is no 'hatch," per se, going on, especially in the Pacific Northwest. How are you going to match the non-existent hatch? I learned to fly fish, and have done 75 percent of my fishing, on the western slope of the Cascades. If you come out here to fish and wait for the hatch to start, you might be waiting a long, long time. Trout in these parts learn to eat what is available, be it insect, salmon egg, or minnow.

Sometimes when a torrid, wild hatch is underway, there are so many naturals on the water that your fly stands very poor mathematical odds just due to the competition. A famous fly fishing author and biologist, Ken Miyata, wrote an influential article titled *Anting the Hatch*. He described the situation above and pointed out the preference that trout show for ants. Throwing an ant pattern in among the feeding trout can result in pulling their attention away from the naturals and the fish grabbing the ant.

Developing Powers of Observation

One of the joys of fly fishing is experiencing the gradual improvement of your powers of observation. At first a lake or stream-side locale presents an overwhelming kaleidoscope of enjoyable visual sensations. Trees and brush; water and the mystery contained in its depths; insects buzzing about; perhaps a rising trout. As you fish, your eyes will start to pick out details and notice things you hadn't seen before. At first all rings on the water's surface you saw as "rises." Later you will learn to differentiate between the rise of a trout and rings on the surface caused by escaping gasses, or a bird ducking under the water, or a salamander surfacing. Later you will discern the difference between the rise of a tiny trout and that of a sizable one, and between a splashy rise to an escaping insect and the gentle, calm rise to an adult mayfly. Your improved powers of observation will help you catch more trout, but also enjoy nature more.

Other Insects Trout Eat

Waterboatmen, backswimmers, crane flies, water beetles, alderflies and dobsonflies are all insects that interest trout at certain times. These are not included in this book for the simple reason that I don't know anything about them. I realize that some would view my reticence due to ignorance as merely a quaint attitude or a manifestation of some neurotic scrupulosity, but I believe readers are better served by my referring them to Chapter 20, *For Further Reading*, which includes several excellent books that will explain the above-mentioned critters, as well as provide much, much more information than I will ever possess on the insects and other food sources of trout.

12. Fly Types Versus Fly Patterns

A *fly pattern* is a specific set of directions and materials for constructing a fly, a recipe if you will. Each is usually referred to by some colorful name, perhaps including reference to the designer, the river of origin, or the insect it represents.

The wide variety of flies developed over the centuries is one of the delights of the sport. Flies have been tied for centuries, and the total number of named fly patterns is unknown but has been estimated to be in the thousands. Traditionally, flies were constructed from a wide variety of animal parts in addition to the hook, thread and possibly a few other non-animal items, such as glue. The animal parts can include feathers, both stiff and soft from a variety of birds; and the body hair of a diverse collection of mammals, such as deer, muskrat, hare, and polar bear. In recent years, a wide range of plastics and other synthetics have been employed, though traditionalists consider this an abomination.

Fly patterns are important, not only for catching fish, but for contributing to the history and traditions of fly fishing. Patterns tell a story about the designer and where and when he or she fished.

A *fly type,* as I use the term, refers to a class of similar fly patterns, designed to be fished in a similar manner. Within each fly type there are thousands of established, named fly patterns, augmented by the efforts of countless experienced anglers who create their own flies without bothering to name them.

To catch fish, it is more important to understand the fly types and their uses, than to catalog countless individual patterns. Fly types are divided into two overall categories: *dry flies*, designed to float on the water's surface, and *wet flies*, designed to sink to various depths of the river or lake.

This distinction between fly patterns and fly types, with the emphasis placed on fly types, has been articulated by many authors: Roderick Haig-Brown and Dave Hughes are two that I am familiar with.

All the flies in this chapter, except the Atlantic salmon flies, were photographed by Gabe Green. For the provenance of the Atlantic salmon flies in this book, see that section.

DRY (FLOATING) FLIES

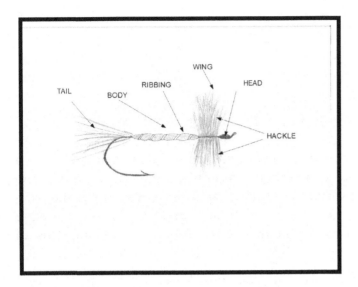

Parts of a typical dry fly

Classic Dry Flies

Dry flies are designed to float on the water's surface and imitate the adult stage of various aquatic insects. To many in the general public, dry flies are what come to mind when fishing flies are mentioned.

To make the fly float, various strategies are employed. The hooks used by dry flies are made of thinner than normal wire - 1X or 2X Fine; the hackle is made of the stiff neck hackle of the male roosters; the tail is long and buoyant. The fly is "dressed" with floatant to repel moisture. Modern fly tiers, breaking with tradition, sometimes construct bodies and/or wings of closed cell foam, little built-in life preservers for the flies.

Dry flies are traditionally fished "dead drift," i.e., floating downstream just as a piece of bark or a cork would. The trick is to make it float as if untethered, i.e., free from the dry fly fisher's all-time bugaboo, "drag."

In contrast to this traditional method, modern anglers have also developed dry fly presentations that conscientiously utilize drag, causing the insect to appear as something alive, dashing to and fro on the surface of the water.

The Adams

Designed by Leonard Halliday from Mayfield, Michigan, in 1922. It represents a wide variety of surface insects, and just plain looks like something good to eat.

Adams

Hook: #12-18, 1X fine
Thread: Black nylon
Tail: Grizzly and brown hackle fibers mixed
Body: Dark gray dubbing
Hackle: Brown and grizzly mixed
Wing: Grizzly hen-hackle tips

Royal Coachman.

Renegade

Light Cahill.

Down-wing Dry Flies

I list the down-wing dry fly as a separate type because of the importance they have held for me in learning to fly fish. Down-wing dry flies typically imitate either a caddis or stonefly adult, both of which fold their wings back across their abdomen when not flying. For the wings, these flies often use elk or deer hair, both of which are hollow and thus act as miniature floatation chambers.

These flies are ideal for fast, rough-and-tumble streams, where traditional dries tend to sink.

Elk-hair Caddis

The Elk-hair Caddis was invented by Al Troth from Pennsylvania in 1957. This fly can be tied in various colors and sizes. For me it has become a go-to dry for rough, broken water.

Elk Hair Caddis

Hook: 1X Fine dry fly hook, size #10 - #16
Thread: Tan
Tail: None
Body: Tan fur, dubbed
Hackle: Ginger, palmered (wound forward from rear of fly to the front)
Wing: Tan elk hair
Ribbing: Fine gold wire

Stimulator.

Bucktail Caddis.

Golden Stone.

Terrestrials

Ant, beetles, grasshoppers, termites; all find themselves blown by the wind onto the surface of lakes and streams. Anglers have for many years devised dry flies to imitate these land-dwelling insects. Because they are helpless, terrestrials are often preferred by trout over other surface insects that have the irritating habit of flying away.

Black Beetle

My dad, Bill Green, Sr., taught me how to tie this fly and, flaunting local fly fishing doctrine, used it to catch rainbows up to 30"at Rocky Ford Creek in Eastern Washington.

Black Beetle

Hook: Dry Fly, 1X fine; size #10-14
Thread: Black
Tail, Body, Head: All made from black deer hair tied in the back then folded over to the front.
Wing: None
Hackle: Black; sparse

Hopper.

Orange Termite.

Flying Ant.

SINKING (WET) FLIES

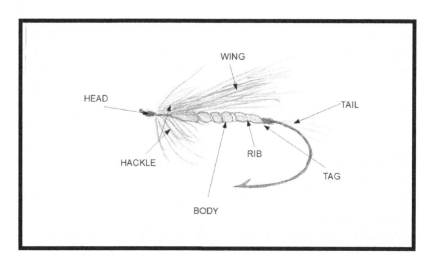

Parts of a typical wet fly.

Soft- Hackles

Soft-hackles are simple yet highly effective wet flies typically fished directly below the surface. They may imitate mayfly or caddis emergers. This fly type is very old, having been developed in the "North Country" in England during the 19th century, as explained in *The Soft-Hackled Fly,* 1975, by Sylvester Nemes.

Soft-hackles are wingless, consisting of no more than a simple floss, yarn, or herl body; a silver or gold ribbing to bind the body to the hook; and hackle from a partridge, starling or other bird with soft, flowing feathers that come alive when subjected to the currents.

This minimalist fly style, seemingly too simple to fool such an intellectual giant as a trout, should be tied in a variety of sizes and colors to approximately match whatever is, or recently has been, hatching.

I do not embark on a fishing trip without a box of soft-hackle flies tied in a variety of sizes and colors in my tackle box.

Partridge and Herl

Hook:	Wet fly hook, #12-14
Thread:	Black
Body:	Peacock herl
Ribbing:	Gold wire
Hackle:	Brown mottled partridge
Head:	Black

Partridge and Yellow and Fur Thorax.

Pheasant Tail.

March Brown Spider.

<u>Classic Wet Flies</u>

Wet flies are among the oldest flies in use. They are designed to sink below the surface and represent sub-surface aquatic insects or possibly small baitfish. Or just look like something good to eat. Early anglers didn't specifically set out to imitate a specific food type but inherited a variety of established named patterns that had proven themselves in their locale.

Blue Dun

This low-key, rather nondescript yet highly effective pattern is tied as either a dry or a wet fly; I learned it as a wet. Originally it was designed to imitate a mayfly of the same name. I think it just looks like a lot of things good to eat, and its low-key, natural appearance doesn't put off the fish with neon lights and blazing brass horns.

Tag: Red

Tail: Blue dun

Body: Dark gray dubbing

Wings: Mallard

Hackle: Blue dun

Mallard and Claret.

March Brown.

Parmachene Belle.

81

<u>Nymphs</u>

In contrast to the rather generic approach of wet flies, modern nymph fishing developed when anglers set out to accurately imitate the larvae, nymph and pupae stages of specific aquatic insects, not just in their physical appearance but also their behavior. This often entailed a fly fished deep below the surface of a stream or lake, a huge departure from traditional fly fishing techniques, even though a large percentage of most trout's diet comes from sub-surface insects.

Bead-headed, Gold-ribbed, Hare's Ear Nymph

Wow, that's a mouthful! By the time you have said the fly's name, the hatch is over. Just call it a Hare's Ear. This is a standard pattern that has been used for at least one-hundred and fifty years, probably longer. It imitates mayfly nymphs or caddis fly pupae, and, like many patterns listed here, it simply resembles something good to eat.

The bead-head is a recent addition, designed to give it some flash as well as weight to sink it down to deep feeding stations. When I learned to tie this fly in the early 1980s, the bead-head concept was not yet popular. Now it seems every other nymph sports a bead-head.

Tied without the bead-head and on a light-wire hook it will fish right below the surface imitating an emerger.

Hook: Wet fly or nymph; size #8 – 16
Thread: Brown
Head: Gold colored brass bead; size to match hook size
Tail: Pheasant tail
Body: Hair from the "mask" of a hare, include guard hairs, spun onto hook
Wing case: Pheasant tail fibers from tail are carried forward and form the wing case

Ribbing: Gold rope

Pheasant Tail.

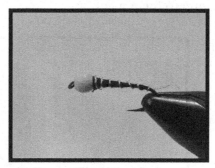
Chironomid.

Copper John.

Streamers

Streamers imitate small fish. A typical streamer will have a silver or gold wire body to imitate the flash of the underside displayed by many fish as they turn in the water. Streamers will also have a long wing to represent the top side of the fish and probably a substantial tail to give the fly the required length.

Streamers have been around a long time. They are typically presented by stripping the fly through the water in quick bursts, six to 12 inches long, but savvy streamer fishermen are not content with this, but instead experiment with varying retrieves until they find what works.

Muddler Minnow

This wacky looking fly was designed by Don Gapin in Michigan. Has become a go-to fly from Oregon to New York. Designed to imitate a sculpin.

Hook: #2 – 6 2X Long Streamer hook
Thread: Tan
Tail: None
Body: Gold ribbing, wrapped to form a continuous gold body
Wing: Tan or rust-red squirrel tail laid first, followed by married turkey quill

Head: Spun deer hair with the forward-pointing hairs trimmed to form a head and the backwards-pointing hairs left long to form a collar

Woolly Bugger

Mickey Finn

Clouser Minnow

Atlantic Salmon Flies

These flies may never grace the end of your leader, but, because of their beauty and historical importance, all anglers should know something about them. In 19th century England and Scotland, salmon fishing was restricted to the nobility. Commoners had to be content with rough fish pursued with bait and lures. The life of a 19th century British aristocrat was one of leisure and pampered luxury. At this time, the British Empire reached its zenith, and aristocratic gentlemen often served as officers in the British army, stationed to far-flung lands such as Burma, India, Egypt, Hong Kong. They returned to their estates and drinking clubs laden with souvenirs, including the feathers of exotic birds: peacock, jungle cock, Chinese pheasant, and ostrich. These were then woven into the beautiful, ornate works of art called Atlantic salmon flies.

There are two types of classic salmon flies: featherwing and hairwing. Hairwing are simpler and utilize materials more readily obtainable. Featherwings are the classic, full-dressed flies as created during the 19th century in England and Scotland.

All the Atlantic salmon flies pictured below and on the cover were tied and photographed by nationally-recognized fly tier Gary Bevers of Woodland, Washington. Gary has invested the considerable time and effort required to master these complex patterns, and the results are breathtaking. (If you are reading a black and white printing of this book, the photographs on these pages will not fully express the beauty of the flies. Please review the book cover for full-color photographs of the Jock Scott on the front and the Green Highlander on the back.)

Jock Scott

The Jock Scott is one of the best-known classic Atlantic salmon flies. It was developed by John (Jock) Scott in about 1850 in Scotland.

Tag: Silver twist and yellow floss silk

Tail: A topping and Indian crow

Butt: Black ostrich herl

Body: Requires two equal halves. The first half is yellow floss butted with black herl, and veiled above and below with six or more Toucan feathers. The second half is black floss.

Ribs: Fine oval silver tinsel over yellow floss, broader oval silver tinsel or flat silver tinsel and twist (in the large sizes) over the black floss

Hackle: A natural black cock's hackle, wound over the black floss

Throat: Speckled Gallina

Wings: A pair of black white-tipped Turkey tail strips (back to back); over these, but not entirely covering them, a "mixed" sheath of "married" strands of Peacock wing, yellow, scarlet, and blue Swan, Bustard, Florican, and Golden Pheasant tail; two strands of Peacock sword feather above; "married" narrow strips Teal and barred Summer Duck at the sides; brown Mallard over.

Sides: Jungle cock

Cheeks: Chatterer

Horns: Blue and yellow macaw

Head: Black ostrich herl

Wow, that's a lot of parts!

Gary's flies are truly works of art. Here are three more:

Blue Jacket.   Green Highlander   Wilson

Attractors

Attractor flies are not designed to imitate available prey, but to provoke fish to strike out of curiosity, anger, or territoriality.

Fish use their mouths for things other than eating. Lacking hands, they grab items of interest with their mouths. Fish also bite other fish, during spawning to repel competing suitors and at other times to maintain their established feeding territories.

When I think of attractors, I think of wet flies, but anglers have also designed attractor dries. Most flies for steelhead, Atlantic salmon, and sea-run cutthroat fishing are attractors.

Spruce

The Spruce was designed around 1918 by brothers Bert and Milo Godfrey of Seaside, Oregon. It catches fish but also is attractive to the angler, which helps explain its decades-long popularity. It quickly became popular for sea-run cutthroat fishing along the Oregon Coast.

The Spruce is an example of what is termed a "breather fly," a fly sporting a pair of splayed feather wings that pulsate in and out as the fly is stripped through the water. To make sure it is working correctly, toss the fly out a few feet in the water and strip it back so that you can see the action. Incidentally, this is a good habit to get into when fishing any wet fly, to see what it really looks like to the fish. One thing you will immediately notice is that wet flies, in the water, look nothing like they do bone-dry, mounted in a showcase in a hardware store. In the water they will typically appear much skinnier.

Spruce.

Hook: Streamer, 3X or 4X long, size 10 to 1/0.
Thread: Black.
Tail: Peacock sword, 3-5 strands, depending on hook size.
Body: Rear 1/3 of red floss; front 2/3 of peacock herl.
Wing: Badger hackle feathers.
Hackle: Badger, tied wet style.

Knudsen Spider (Yellow).

Green Butt Skunk.

Brad's Brat.

A Baker's Dozen Flies for the Pacific Northwest

From the thirty-eight flies photographed above I have selected a good all-around collection for fishing throughout the Pacific Northwest. Tied in different sizes, some weighted some unweighted, the thirteen flies identified below easily becomes 50 or more choices, plenty enough to fool a trout.

Dry Flies:

1. Adams
2. Royal Coachman
3. Elk-hair Caddis
4. Beetle-popper
5. Stimulator

Wet Flies:

6. Partridge and Herl Soft-hackle
7. Iron-blue Dun
8. Hare's-ear Nymph
9. Pheasant-tail Nymph
10. Copper John
11. Muddler Minnow
12. Woolly Bugger
13. Spruce

One particularly slow winter evening, bereft of other entertainment or amusement, I inventoried my flies. I determined that I was the proud owner of about 250 flies representing about 90 unique patterns. All the above fly types, except Atlantic salmon flies, were well represented. I know that my collection is dwarfed by those possessed by many experienced anglers. But what amazes me is how many experienced anglers I know that may own 200 or more patterns but end up doing most of their fishing with just a handful of go-to flies.

13. Presenting the Fly in Moving Water

Presentation refers to the way the fly is seen by the fish. After the fly lands on the water, actions that affect the presentation include line mending (described below), a variety of line retrieves, and rod positioning and movement during the drift.

Stealth

Stealth should be a cornerstone of any presentation of a fly to fish. Fish, trout in particular, survive by avoiding predators such as anglers, birds, and their older siblings. **Scared fish cannot be caught.** Sometimes when an animal is scared it will "bolt" for cover, a rapid, dramatic flight for its life. But, in a response less well understood, often a trout will not bolt when spooked but instead hunker down, nervous, avoiding your fly.

Wade slowly and carefully. Always fish a patch of water before you wade into it (better, don't wade into it). Wear drab clothes. Avoid banging your feet on the rocks. Stay back from the water where you are casting. Strive to cast so that the fly lands softly on the water.

While it is true that sounds originating above the water do not continue below the water's surface, it's best to speak softly, even if only to avoid bothering fellow anglers. A good rule to follow as far as etiquette is "when in Rome do as the Romans"; if there are specific rules of etiquette that anglers follow in a given place, they most likely have been worked out there for good reasons and you should try to follow them.

> *I encountered an example of local etiquette while fishing with my brother Bill on Idaho's famed Silver Creek, a demanding, slow-moving spring creek with large, spooky trout. As we began to fish I called out to him from about ten yards away. Bill responded with "shhhhh" with his index finger to his lips. I thought this strange, since sound does not carry underwater, but I was the visitor and I took his advice. Everyone there maintained the quite of a library. Later, I observed a group of large birds spook and fly off. It occurred to me that the birds may have heard a loud noise and responded with flight, and that the wary trout below the water may have seen the bird's reaction and perhaps spooked as well.*

An axiom I follow is "if you can see the fish, the fish has already spotted you." I can't prove this, but I believe it is true. Yet anglers "sight-fish" and authors promote sight-fishing techniques. Sight-fishing is defined as first visually searching the water for fish using polarized sun glasses, then presenting the fly to the identified fish. The obvious advantage is that the angler knows he is casting to a fish, in contrast to fishing in general in which you often are casting through water without knowing whether or not it holds fish. The disadvantage is that the fish has already spotted you. My personal opinion, not shared by all, is that sight fishing is generally a waste of time. I have watched anglers spot a fish and then cast repeatedly over it, sometimes for hours, without moving the fish. Wouldn't it make more sense to move on and find a fish that is willing to bite?

> *I've done it myself, and here is something I learned. Years ago I was lure-fishing for steelhead and salmon on the Lewis River. I spotted a group of salmon and began casting to them. No response, I changed lures, kept trying, kept trying. My lure was drifting right by their snouts.*
>
> *After a half hour or so of this, I noticed something. The fish and I had been doing a slow downstream dance together. I was drifting my lure right to them and they just calmly*

moved downstream a little to avoid the lure, which clearly bothered them. Now we were about 30-40 feet downstream from our starting point. The lesson here is that just because a fish does not bolt, does not mean the fish is not spooked. These fish were spooked before I ever cast the lure.

Another dimension of stealth is smell. Recall that a trout's sense of smell is so acute as to boggle our minds. Before you tie flies, or handle your flies or leader, be sure to wash your hands thoroughly. If you fill up with gas on the way out be especially sure to remove all traces of petroleum scent from your hands. Some anglers like to rub their fingers and their flies through the sand along shore in order to remove scents as well as possibly add some local scent.

WET FLY PRESENTATIONS

Wet flies sink. Sometimes deep, sometimes almost in the surface film, sometimes stripped furiously through the water, sometimes teased slowly across the currents.

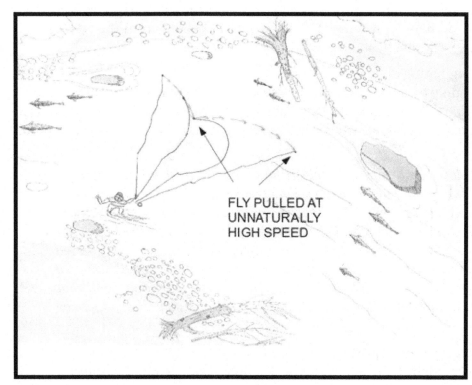

FLY PULLED AT UNNATURALLY HIGH SPEED

Some consider wet fly techniques easier to learn than dry fly. I consider this a dubious proposition at best. Certainly wet fly techniques are not easier to achieve full mastery (if this is ever achieved).

I spend about 85 percent of my fishing time with sunk flies, and I would expect that percentage to be common among other anglers in the Pacific Northwest.

Line Mending

To understand wet fly fishing in moving water one must understand line mending. *It is the heart and soul of fishing a wet fly.*

To "mend" the line is to re-position the line or parts of the line during the downstream drift of the fly. The result is controlling the drift or "swim" of the fly. Changing it from an unnaturally fast slap of the fly around on a tight pull, see "crack the whip" above, to a natural, enticing "swim" of the fly, gradually being coaxed across the river.

Mending is done both with wet fly and dry fly presentations. The purpose is to correct or improve the drift of the fly. In dry fly fishing, it is usually done to eliminate drag. With the wet fly it is done to slow the fly down and eliminate unnatural dragging of the fly.

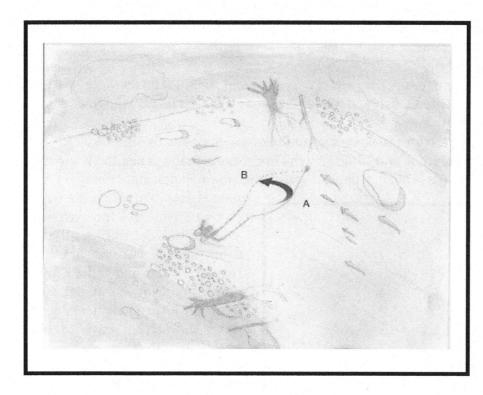

Line mending.

As a new fly fisher, I read several books that explained line mending, but I did not grasp its purpose. Also, at that time I was struggling with the basics of casting and so decided I could learn about mending later.

Then on a fine summer day, I took my young family on a picnic to Moulton Falls State Park on the East Fork Lewis River. We enjoyed barbecued hamburgers and admired the beauty of the waterfalls. We found a small side pool where the kids could safely splash and wade. Later, I snuck upstream with my fly rod and found a broad flow of even current. Something made me want to experiment with this thing called "mending." I cast a wet fly across the stream, and as the current began to pull the belly of the line ahead of the fly, the fly began to speed up. I mended the belly back upstream, and watched the fly slow down, returning to a nice, gentle swimming across the current. Then , as the belly began to form again, I repeated the mend.

I was enthralled. I had an epiphany. I could make the fly do what I wanted it to do.

Before this day, what I had been doing was letting the belly of the line speed the fly into a "crack the whip" effect.

For an hour, I cast the fly and experimented with mending and controlling the drift of the fly: mending upstream, mending downstream, changing the casting angle, carefully studying the drift or "swim" of the fly.

*All at once that afternoon, I understood not only the importance of mending but, more broadly, **the importance of being in control of the line**, and therefore in control of the path and speed of the fly.*

Wet Fly I: Swinging a Wet Fly

Swinging a wet fly down and across the current is an excellent way to search water. By casting and swinging the fly in an arc, then stepping down one stride and repeating, large swaths of good looking holding water can be searched. To obtain an enticing motion of the fly, mending, usually multiple mends per cast, is essential.

Swinging the wet fly, step by step:

- Cast across or at an angle downstream, depending on the current;
- Immediately mend upstream;

- Whenever a line begins to form a belly, mend upstream. Mend as many times as you need to keep the line from forming a bow;
- Follow the line with your rod tip;
- When the line is directly downstream, the drift is over, but you can hold the fly there "hanging" for a few seconds. Often a fish will follow the fly as it makes its way down and across, and strike at this point;
- Now retrieve the line to prepare for the next cast, and take a step downstream.

Many books of fly fishing describe mending and some give the impression that it is needed when the line crosses currents of varying speeds. This is true, and for upstream presentations it may be the main reason. But when the fly is cast across or downstream, even if the current is all the same speed there is another reason. A line allowed to drift downstream of the angler will naturally form an arc in order to cross the stream back to the angler. In our example in the diagram to the left, the distance the arc travels at the end of the line, is twice the distance traveled by the arc directly at the end of the rod. With no correcting action the Crack the Whip effect occurs. Mending makes up the difference and prevents unnatural drag.

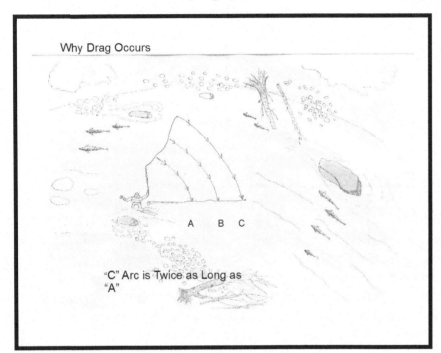

What to do with the fly rod while the fly is drifting downstream? A starting point is to point the rod tip at the fly and follow it around until it is directly below you. But there are nuances to this, and the angler should study the effect of changes in rod position on the drift of the line.

Wet Fly II: Greased Line

One of my favorite books on fly presentation is *Greased Line Fishing for Salmon*, based on the notebooks of A.H.E. Wood. It was written by "Jock Scott," pen-name of Donald G. Ferris Rudd.

Arthur Wood, an English gentleman and engineer who died in 1934, developed techniques for presenting a sparsely tied wet fly within an inch or two of the surface to Atlantic salmon. Other anglers have taken these techniques and applied them in pursuit of steelhead, sea-run cutthroat, and resident trout.

The equipment for greased line fishing is a double-taper floating line, a tapered floating leader, and an unweighted wet fly. The fly is cast across river, the angle varying depending on currents. The fly remains in or near the surface film. The line is frequently mended with the goal of keeping the fly just barely working against the current, thus being subjected to the varied currents. For much of the drift, the fly is presented to the fish broadside, providing a larger image to the fish.

To me, greased line is more of an approach rather than a specific technique. In practice, experienced anglers fish wet flies using a flexible blend of the wet fly swing and greased line. This approach places line handling at the forefront and fly selection on the back burner.

Here is a description of the greased line technique from Arthur Wood himself *(Greased Line Fishing for Salmon,* page 63)

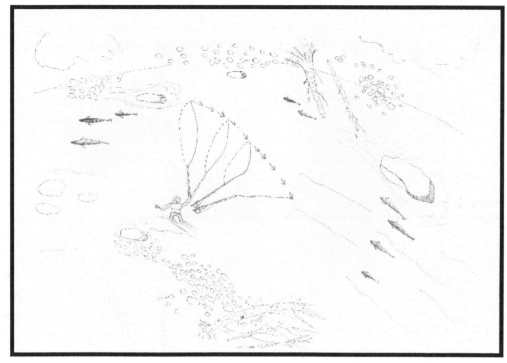

Typical Greased Line Drift

"The basic idea is to use the line as a float for, and controlling agent of, the fly; to suspend the fly just beneath the surface of the water, and to control its path in such a way that it swims diagonally down and across the stream, entirely free from the slightest pull of the line."

Fish Following a Swinging Fly

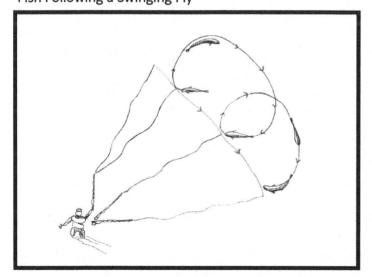

Arthur Wood fills his book with useful nuggets gleaned from his years of careful observation of fish and the fly. One is found on page 67. It demonstrates a fish following a swinging fly, and circling several times as it looks and perhaps nibbles at the fly. When I first read this I thought it a bit fanciful and wondered how the author would know this.

Several years later I fished for steelhead on the lower Deschutes with my friend Todd Calvin. Todd is a natural athlete who played collegiate baseball, and his long, graceful wet fly casts across the classic steelhead drift I admired with perhaps a tinge of jealousy. By late afternoon he had landed two steelhead and hooked and lost a third, while I had nothing. Wanting to see what he was doing that worked so well, I climbed up a small berm above the drift he was fishing. He was casting the same pattern as I was, through the same drift I had fished without result. The fly swam down and across the drift. From my position above him I clearly saw a steelhead follow the fly, nip at it, turn away, circle around, follow again, nip again, circle a third time. By this time the fly was nearly directly below Todd, and the fish grabbed the fly this time hooking himself. After a spirited battle a five-pound steelhead lay at his feet.

Just as Mr. Wood said.

Nymphing

Wet flies imitate a variety of organisms and also act as attractor flies. In contrast, modern nymphing developed as a specific attempt to imitate the nymph, pupae and larvae stages of aquatic insects.

The Deep-Sunk Nymph

Trout do most of their feeding sub-surface, and often deep down in the stream. Nymphs and larvae of aquatic insects, as well as salmonid eggs, become dislodged from their holds on the bottom and drift downstream near the river bottom. The basic technique for drifting a nymph deeply in a drag-free manner starts with an upstream cast of a weighted nymph, often aided by a small bobber to help control the drift and detect a strike.

A variety of rigs have been developed for the deep-sunk nymph. Each of these was developed by experienced anglers for specific stream situations. To gain mastery of nymphing the angler needs to experiment with these rigs and try them over a variety of situations and learn what works where.

Three possible nymph rigs.

If you were to take a weighted nymph, or another object of similar size and density, and toss it into the water upstream, untethered, it would sink to the bottom in a surprisingly short distance. When we cast the same nymph upstream we struggle to get it to sink deeply. Why? Obviously, it is tethered to the leader, which pulls on the fly and slows its rate of sink. The answer to sinking the fly deep is to eliminate this pulling. One way to do this is to throw a slack line cast. This can be achieved by waving the rod tip as the line is straightening out in front of you on the forward cast. This helps, but after it sinks a bit the slack is consumed and the pull of the line acts on the fly. Add to the slack line, casting the line and leader **above** the fly. Then, during the drift, mend the line to keep the line above the fly. This is where the bobber helps. This is called a **"button-hook mend."**

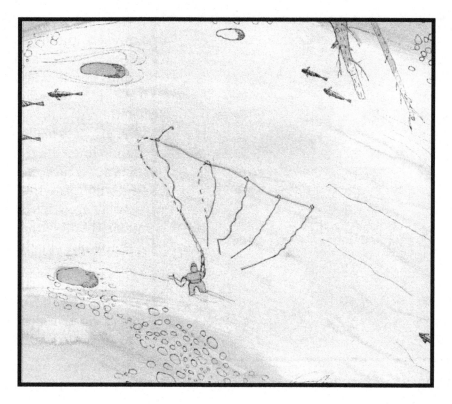

As the fly drifts downstream, gaining depth, the fly is also getting closer to the angler, so what to do with all of that extra line? If you let it accumulate, and you get a strike, you will have difficulty setting the hook and playing the fish. You could strip it in. Or, you could lift your rod straight up, absorbing the extra line. Then as the fly passes below you, reverse the process and lower you rod tip, feeding the line back into the drift, thus extending the drift and allowing the fly to drift deep. This is called **"high-sticking."**

Buttonhook mend.

DRY FLY PRESENTATIONS

Dry Fly I: The Upstream Dry Fly

Toss a piece of bark upstream and watch it float back to you. Untethered to any line, it will float downstream, following the variegated currents drag -free. Many insects at times behave this way, and the upstream dry fly imitates that behavior.

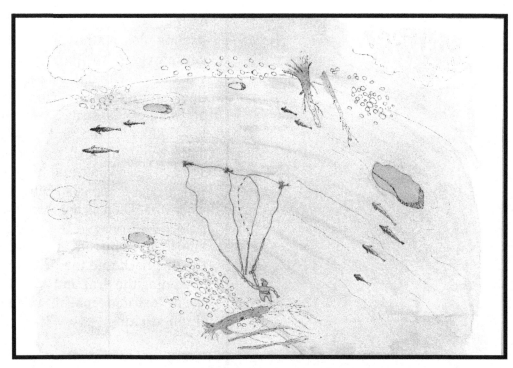

Upstream dry presentation.

The challenge is to present the fly as if free and untethered, when it is in fact tethered to a length of leader and line. If the currents are not uniform–they rarely are where I fish–then either the leader, in the faster current will drag the fly, or the fly, in the faster current, will drag against the leader.

Here are some tools to overcome drag:

– add some slack line into the cast;
– mend the line, either upstream or downstream;
– re-position the fly mid-drift;
– abandon the spot and fish from another location. There are casting spots from which it is difficult or impossible to get a good drift. Move on.

The upstream dry fly imitates the mayfly dun drying its wings in preparation for flight and also many terrestrial insects that float helplessly downstream.

Dry Fly II: The Downstream Dry Fly

The dry fly can also be presented dead drift downstream. To do this, at the start of the drift hold the rod up high, then as the fly drifts downstream, lower your rod tip at the speed of the current, thus allowing the fly to proceed downstream dead drift. This presentation has the advantage of presetting the fly before the leader and line thus eliminating any spooking of fish due to the leader and line.

Downstream Dry Presentation

Dry Fly III: The Active Dry Fly

Sometimes insects floating on the surface don't sit still and behave themselves. Like kindergartners lining up for recess, they hop and jump around.

Until in the 1970s, dry fly fishing was dominated by the upstream, dead-drift dogma. Then several authors expanded anglers' mindsets. Leonard Wright wrote several books in the 1970s, including *Fishing the Dry Fly as a Living Insect* and *Fly Fishing Heresies.* Wright explained that many insects, in particular caddisflies, do not sit motionless on the surface, but are active, both in their emergence and the egg-laying phases.

Techniques for the active dry fly include skating and twitching the fly across the surface. The downstream dry fly presentation portrayed above provides a starting point. While the fly is drifting down drag-free, add an upstream twitch. When the fly has reached the end of the drift and your rod tip is nearly horizontal, instead of re-casting, just raise the rod tip back up to a nearly vertical position and repeat the drift without a back cast. Experiment. Let the fly skate across the surface under drag. Pop the fly across the surface throwing up a wake. You might be surprised by a violent rise. If not, after a while, try something else.

14. Striking, Playing, and Handling Fish

The word "strike" has two meanings in fishing. Strike refers to the fish gobbling up the fly or lure. The second meaning is the response of the angler who may tighten or pull back on the line to ensure that the fly has found a solid hold in the fish's mouth.

The way a fish strikes depends on many variables: Is he striking in anger or feeding? Is the line and leader tight between the fly and the angler or is there slack line, is the fly deep below the surface or on the surface? All of these will affect how the fish strikes and how you feel (or don't feel) the strike.

When a fish takes a fly, he immediately senses that it is bogus and quickly expels the fly, if he can. With bait fishing, the fish tastes the bait and is fooled for a longer period of time. A key skill is to sense when the fish is on the line and quickly respond by tightening the line before the fish can expel the fly. Keep in mind that fish sometime strike hard and sometimes not. When they strike hard they often hook themselves and you don't need to do anything. But because they sometimes strike gently, or if you are fishing deep and it is harder to detect a strike, your ability to sense the strike is a skill that you should hone.

So how do you strike when you feel the fish? Just a quick pulling back of the tip of the rod to tighten the line and set the hook. Bait fisherman often like to reef back, pulling the tip from a three o'clock to a noon or 11 o'clock position. But they are often fishing deep. Using a bobber on the surface with the fly running deep is a time-honored technique to aid in strike detection that fly fisherman stole from bait fisherman back in the 1960s. By watching the bobber as it drifts downstream, any unnatural movement of the bobber signal that the angler should set the hook.

The first few fish the beginning angler catches probably struck quite hard. That was certainly the case with me. The reason is obvious: I missed all the fish that struck lightly! It is easy for a beginner to begin to believe that fish always strike hard because the fish they catch strike hard. The problem is they missed all the gentle takes.

Now that you've hooked the trout you need to play it. This is generally the easiest and most enjoyable aspect of the sport. The key concept is to **always keep tension on the line, never let it go limp.** To do this hold the rod high and let the tip of the rod absorb the fish's pulling on the line. If you have a large fish, it's usually better and more fun to play it from the reel. You need to wind in all the slack line that may have collected, then crank the fish in directly from the reel. For small fish, you probably don't want to bother winding in the slack. Just strip in the line through your fingers of your right hand.

The real devil-fish to play is one that swims directly toward you. At least to me, this happens most often in lake fishing. There is no way you can reel in fast enough to keep up with this fish. If you don't keep up with the fish, you will have slack line and the fish will take the opportunity and end his relationship with you at that point. So you need to **strip in line as fast as you can**, hoping and praying that you can maintain constant tension on the line.

Now you have the fish of your dreams and he runs away from you. This is when the drag on the reel comes in and adds tension to the line peeling off the reel. Don't try to stop that big fish's first powerful run. Let him go and wear himself out. It is the fish's running and jumping that wears it out and allows you to land him.

When to land the fish? When the pull of the line is lifting his head out of the water. Now you have the fish nearly in hand. If you are going to release the fish, you need to minimize handling the fish and try not to take him out of the water at all. I usually do not use a net; instead I reach down, grab the fly and yank it out of the fish's jaw and he's free to go. If the fly is hard to get out, I reach into my vest and pull out my needle-nose pliers and let them do the work. If you are using a net, remember to hold the net about half in and half out of the water and don't move the net, instead pull the fish head-first into the net. When he's in there just lift the net and he's yours.

I hope you will **release all wild fish**, at least. Remember to handle the fish as little as possible and keep the fish in the water as much as possible and minimize the time the fish is captured and therefore unable to breath. You may also need to revive a fish prior to release to ensure that it will live. If you are fishing in moving water, hold the fish in the current, allowing the water to flow past the fish's gills thus reviving it. Don't release it until you feel its strength returning and it fights its way out of your hands. In still water you may need to cradle the fish and slowly move it back and forth in the water so that the water flows over its gills and again wait till its strength returns and it swims away under its own power.

If you are going to harvest the fish, the way to kill it is to hit it on the head with a stout stick or a rock. Do not use a stringer. Stringers are inhumane and should be illegal. Putting a fish on a stringer causes the fish to spend hours in agony, half dead and half alive, with the vague notion of "keeping the fish fresh." Last year I witnessed an angler land a ten-pound steelhead, place it on a stringer, and "secure" the other end of the stringer with a pile of rocks. The fish uprooted the stringer from the rock pile and swam away from shore dragging a three-foot length of chain. A testament to the fish's strength and determination and to the stupidity of the "sportsman" who did it. That fish won't last long in the wild tethered to a three-foot length of chain.

15. A Lake Fishing Primer

For most of the long history of fly fishing, lake fishing has taken back-seat to stream fishing. I am not sure why. Even today, the output of angling literature devoted to streams far outweighs that of lake fishing. But steadily since World War II lake fishing has gained in popularity, and today there are many fine books devoted to the subject.

Don't overlook lakes. Fishing lakes will allow you to expand the number of months in an average year that you can find decent fishing. Pacific Northwest streams are often closed during the spring to protect spawning fish, and often unfishable due to the "spring runoff," which is the annual melting of headwaters' snowpack and the resulting flooding of rivers.

And in lakes you will often find bigger trout. Trout have more to eat in most lakes than in the typical Pacific Northwest freestone stream, thus they can grow larger.

Perhaps lakes do not look as inviting to the angler as a river. I was at first drawn exclusively to river fishing by the beauty of the flowing water: riffles, deep mysterious pools, waterfalls, it's all mesmerizing. I could wade into a stream and work downstream anticipating that around each bend I would discover unexpected visual treats.

A lake is a little harder to appreciate. At first glance it looks the same everywhere. Where do you start? Where are the fish? But look a little closer, spend some time with a lake, and her secrets will slowly unfold. You will notice the shallows, weed beds, inlet creeks, perhaps an ancient creek bed. Small protected bays can harbor unseen jewels. The wide sameness gives way to a garden of opportunities.

Where to start?

Below is a map of Merrill Lake, a 280 acre, fly fishing only lake situated at 1,250 feet elevation in Southwest Washington. It illustrates many important features found in lakes.

> **Outlet Creek:** Water flows into a lake and therefore must flow out. It may flow out in the form of one or more visible outlet creeks, or the water may flow underground. This lake was formed when lava flows from an ancient eruption of Mount St. Helens blocked the path of "Merrill Creek," which had, up to that time, flowed northwards about three or four miles to join the Kalama River. Now a marshy area at the north end of the lake feeds into a slow-moving creek that winds its way to the Kalama River.

> **Weed beds**: An area rich in insect life. Cast along the edge of the weeds and you may be in for a surprise.

> **Shallows:** Shallows produce food for trout, and you don't need to go deep to find the fish. This area also has a muddy bottom. Burrowing mayflies, such as the Hexagenia, need a muddy bottom for the nymphs to develop in; in July Merrill is famous for its "Hex," or Hexagenia, mayfly hatch.

Island: In the high water of spring this island is completely submerged. As spring turns to summer and the water recedes the vegetation provides a nice food-rich holding spot. Also a great place to get hung up if you row your boat over it.

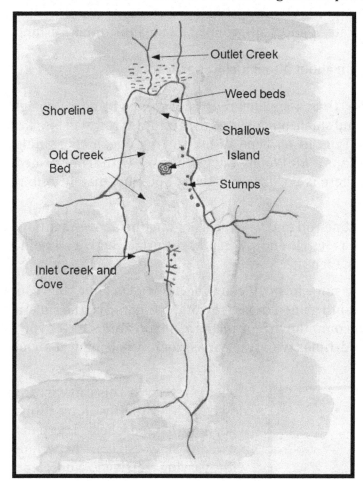

Stumps: There is a row of old drowned trees reaching above the water one to six feet. These provide excellent cover for trout. Also, great places to high-center a boat if you are not careful.

Inlet Creek and Cove: The presence of inlet creeks in a lake herald promise for natural production of trout. That is because trout spawn in moving water and an inlet stream can provide spawning habitat. This lake has several year-round creeks. Also, the inlet bays provide protection from the wind.

Old Creek Bed: By tracing the depths of the lake from the outlet southward to the end of the lake one can identify the old "Merrill Creek" river bed.

Shoreline: Because it is long and thin with numerous coves, this lake has a lot of shoreline. Many folks I talk to seem to think that the deepest parts of the lake are where the fish are hiding. Actually the shoreline, weed beds, and areas of relatively shallow water support more food for trout than the depths of the lake.

Your favorite lake may not have all of the above features, but probably many, and perhaps a few that Merrill lacks. Not all lakes have inlet creeks; the primary water source for many small lakes is underwater springs. That doesn't mean such a lake cannot offer good fishing, it just means that there won't be any wild trout, except brook trout, who can spawn in still water. The lake may be stocked with trout or it may host panfish or bass, both of which can spawn in the shallows of a lake or pond and can offer excellent fly fishing.

Sinking Lines

To fish lakes successfully, the new angler should purchase one or more full-sinking lines. If fish are not feeding on the surface of a lake, to catch fish you must get down to where they are. Full sinking lines are tailor-made for lake fishing because the lake's absence of current allows a deeply sunk line to probe the depths without being buffeted and twisted about by the currents found in a river.

Sinking lines are classified according to their sink rate in inches per second:

Type I: 1.25 to 2 inches per second sink rate. Sometimes termed "intermediate lines", this line is designed to get your fly just below the surface. Often these lines are transparent to aid in a stealthy approach.

Type II: Sinks at about 1 to 2 inches per second.

Type III: 3.5 to 4.5 inches per second sink rate. A good, all-around sinking line for lake fishing.

Type IV, V and VI: Sink at rates ranging from about 4 to 8 inches per second.

I like to carry two fly rods when I fish a lake: One, a smaller rod, say a 5-weight or a 4-weight, matched with a floating line, nine-foot leader, and small, unweighted fly. The other rod, will be a little heavier, usually a 6-weight, equipped with a Type III or Type IV full-sinking line, a short, quick-tapering leader, and probably a larger fly, perhaps a #8 Woolly Bugger to start with. Thus armed, I can probe the depths with the sinking line if there is no surface activity, but immediately grab the floating line rod if surface activity heats up.

An obvious alternative to carrying two rods is one rod and two reels holding the above-mentioned lines. For me, the problem with this approach is impatience. When I see surface activity, I tend to want to keep fishing and not take the time to change rigs.

Sinking line techniques usually are built around some form of "counting down": Cast out, then count a chosen number of seconds, say twenty. The depth gained can be roughly estimated by the sink rate of your line times the number of seconds you count down. For instance, if you are using a Type III line which sinks at about four inches per second, times twenty seconds, your fly is fishing at about a six-foot depth.

Photo by John Geyer.

Then the retrieve. This can vary from slowly inching the fly along to mad, wild, foot-long dashes. Try pauses between slow strips. Experiment with varying retrieves and depths until you strike pay dirt. Like the old football adage, change a losing strategy and maintain a winning strategy.

Years ago my dad taught me an excellent sinking line technique that could be termed the "bonus drift." Cast the sinking line as far as you are able, then peel off twenty or thirty feet of line and flip it out into the water towards the fly. Then slowly row away from your cast until the extra line is almost straightened out. Then count down as described above to allow the fly to reach the desired depth. Now retrieve the line. This will allow your fly to stay in the "zone" longer, and, since each cast is at least 20-30 feet from the preceding cast, allow you to cover more water.

Boats

Realistically, to fish most lakes effectively, some sort of water-craft is needed. Trying to work your way around the shoreline on foot, fighting shoreline brush and trees, sinking into boggy ground, etc., is usually a lesson in frustration.

There are advantages and disadvantages of the various boating options and you should consider several questions before selecting:

- What lakes do you intend to fish? Large or small; what is the lake access, drive to the edge, hike in, boat ramp?
- Do you usually fish by yourself or with companions?
- What level of discomfort are you willing to endure?

Here are some quick, general guidelines:

Float-tube: Can carry to lakeside, don't need a truck to transport, but rather uncomfortable–you are submerged in the water. Limited in the distance you may travel.

Pontoon Boat: A big step up in comfort from a float tube, but short of a real boat, easy to transport, easy to inflate. A few are designed for two persons, but most just for one.

Car-top Boat: Stay dry and comfortable, can cover more distance than in a float-tube, can possibly add a trolling motor, may need a truck to transport, may be able to carry a short distance by using a dolly.

Canoe: Rather tippy, which limits their appeal to the fly angler.

Full-sized motorboat with trailer: Can travel longer distances on a big lake, require more logistics and effort to get in the water. Tough for the solo angler.

Kayak: During the last five to ten years, kayaks have become popular for fly fishing. I have not had the chance to try one out. Several websites are dedicated to the subject; they would be a good place to start.

On a fine June evening, I rowed away from the boat launch at Merrill Lake and headed north towards a picket fence of tree stumps that skirted the shoreline for a couple of hundred yards. A gentle breeze rippled the surface of the water and refreshed me after the heat of afternoon. The snow had melted from the surrounding hills. Now recovering from an earlier clear-cut, the hillsides were now bathed in the green of new growth. The spring water was still high in the lakeside brush, and a hatch of tiny insects flirted about its edge. Not a sound. I let out some line and trolled a fly behind the boat.

I've never subscribed to the doctrine that each and every minute you are fishing your mind must be fully absorbed with the catching of fish, blocking out all distractions. I indulge in many such distractions: enjoying the beauty of the surrounding hills, considering the amazing diversity of nature, possibly offering a small prayer of thanksgiving for all that I see.

Looking northward, I saw the outlet of the lake, a marshy field extending over perhaps 10 acres. Behind it, gentle, rolling hills masked the lava flows that blocked the creek, formed the lake, flowed down the Kalama River valley, and destroyed everything in its path. I pondered; how long ago was the eruption that formed Merrill Lake?

The most recent eruption of Mount St. Helens in May, 1980, resulted in at least two new lakes: Coldwater Lake and Castle Lake, both directly north of the mountain in the Toutle River drainage. Both are popular fly fishing lakes, both formed by a lava flow blocking a creek, just like Merrill Lake.

One of the Native American names for Mount St. Helens is Loowit. One of their legends holds that Loowit was a beautiful maiden, and that Wy'east (Mount Hood, 60 miles south) and Klickitat (Mount Adams, 35 miles east) were young, ardent suitors. Loowit dallied between the two suitors, thus angering the gods, who, in a fit of impatient rage, turned all three into volcanic peaks.

My reveries were interrupted by an angry tug on my fly line followed by a few feet of line pulling off the reel, followed by the line going limp.

Now the sun was setting, the wind stilled, and an eerie calm enveloped the lake. A fish rose near shore. Then, in an instant, the setting sun turned the water's surface into a shimmering sheet of flame. Moments later, darkness.

Did I catch any fish that evening? Just can't remember.

16. Safety

I doubt whether outdoor safety is a topic that results in a lot of New York Times bestsellers. But there are a few topics that are critical.

Eye Protection

A few years ago, a teenage boy from our church parish expressed a strong interest in learning to fly fish and tie flies. We tied some basic flies, then I took him to a lake for some casting practice. I got him started and all seemed to be going well. Like I do with anyone so unfortunate to have me as an instructor I yelled at him for a while, exhorting him to keep a tight casting loop. When my voice became hoarse, I let him practice on his own and I began to cast myself. As I said, all was going per plan.

Suddenly, I heard a scream from his direction. He was holding his hand over his eye and yelling out in pain. I ran over to him. His backcast had caught him in the cheek about one or two inches below his right eye. The #12 barbless hook came out easily. He was fine, more startled than hurt.

I was more than a little startled. From that point forward I have ensured that I or anyone fishing under my tutelage has eye protection at all times. You cannot go onto the internet and order a spare eyeball. You only get two and they are not replaceable.

Wading Safety

Like casting and mending, wading is a necessary, basic skill. Streams vary widely in the degree of wading difficulty. Sandy bottom rivers are usually relatively easy to navigate. Fast rivers with bottoms consisting of large, slick rocks and sudden drop-offs can represent the other end of the spectrum. I have often thought that rivers should have a rating system such as is used for kayaking: Class I, Class II, etc.

So don't start your wading on the most difficult stream.

Proper gear for wading includes three basics:

- Either felt soled or nail-bottomed wading shoes
- A stout wading staff
- A wading belt

To wade safely, move slowly, and tentatively extend your foot forward, feeling the river bottom to find a solid grip. Don't commit your weight onto your extending foot until you have found a spot that will give you decent traction. Your weight should remain on the other two points, the wading staff and your stationary foot. Then gingerly transfer weight to the extending foot.

Don't try to go too fast.

Boating Safety

The importance of boating safety should be obvious to any reader. Every year people drown, not just in huge storms, far out at sea, but in the placid waters of your local streams and lakes with fine weather overhead.

One rule of thumb often quoted is the "50-50-50" rule: If the water temperature is 50 degrees, and the person is 50 yards from shore with no life preserver, he or she has a 50 percent chance of surviving by swimming to shore. Those aren't good odds. In the spring, the temperatures of many lakes and rivers holding trout are not even fifty degrees.

If you have not recently taken a recognized boater safety course, you should by all means do so before launching your boat. These courses are taught by a wide variety of organizations. In many states they are now required in order to legally operate a boat over a certain size.

Part 3: Beyond the Basics

17. Strategies and Tactics

This chapter is a grab-bag of principles I have learned during my forty-odd years of fly fishing. These "rules" hold true about 90 percent of the time. You will come to see when they don't hold and you will find "exceptions that prove the rule."

Don't expect to learn to fly fish in one year

It took me a year and a half to catch my first trout on a fly, a ten-inch, hatchery rainbow. It took me at least five years before I felt I had attained basic competency in casting, reading water, wading, etc. After five years, I still knew almost nothing about insects or hatches. In our world of instant gratification, we often don't grasp that things worth learning take time and commitment. Fly fishing can be enjoyed at many levels of competency, and as the years go by and our skills increase, our appreciation for the sport should deepen.

Fishing the hatch versus fishing the water

When insects are hatching and fish are rising to them, you know where the fish are. You may or may not be successful in hooking them, but they have betrayed their location. With no hatching insects, with a trout's legendary ability to hide underwater, how do you know where the trout are? You can learn where the likely spots are, but you don't know for sure.

When there is no hatch, you are "fishing the water." In the western portion of the Pacific Northwest this means **most the time**. When fishing the water, you must move and find the fish, or more accurately, find the feeding fish.

Which leads to the next strategy:

Get a move-on

This advice is based on my own experience as well as comparing beginning anglers and experienced anglers. Once on the river or lake, beginners tend to stay put; experienced anglers keep moving until they find fish. Whether you are on a stream or a lake, most of the water contains no fish, therefore you must move to find the fish.

In stream-fishing, one approach is: cast – step – cast – step. In this manner, you methodically search the water. Can be done either upstream or downstream.

After fishing for an hour or so, think back, how much real estate did you cover? If you stayed in one spot, and caught no fish, then consider that *there may have been no fish at that spot to catch.*

Should you cover all the water? No. There are sections that are impossible or difficult or dangerous to fish, so skip them. Also, I will pass over water in which I can clearly see the bottom and there is no "cover" i.e., no objects such as large rocks or branches the fish can hide around. Fish make it their business to hide from predators (you), so you normally won't see them.

Fish from the inside of curves in a river

Consider that most rivers curve back and forth for much of their course. The insides of the curves make the logical places to fish, for a couple of reasons: (1) Usually the inside bank will gently slope into deeper water, while the outside edge will drop off quickly into deep, fast current making wading impossible; and (2) Fishing the inside curve, the fast water will be on the opposite side. Recall the discussion of "crack the whip" and the need to eliminate dragging the fly downstream. The inside curve of the river automatically minimizes these problems, while fishing from the opposite bank *magnifies* them.

If the river runs straight for a distance, often the fast current will run along one bank; fish from the other side, and you probably will find a gentle bank to wade out on and cast towards the fast water.

When lake-fishing, get a boat or other craft, and set up two fly rods, one with a sinking line and the other a floater

Fishing from the shore of a lake, *in most situations*, severely hampers your ability to cover water and find feeding fish. There are notable exceptions, and if you have access to a lake fishery where experienced anglers successfully fish from shore, by all means follow their lead. But these exceptions prove the rule.

Rigging up two rods allows you flexibility of presentation. If you go with just a floating line, much of the time you are just getting casting practice; the fish are deeper down and the sink line will get you to them. My experience with hatches on lakes is that they come on quickly and if you must stop and re-rig your rod with a floater and floating fly, the hatch may be over by the time you get the line over the fish.

Cultivate Many Sources of Angling Intelligence

A successful fishing trip involves: the right place – the right time – the right techniques. To plan a successful trip, you should gather as much information as you can. When I started fishing, a major source of information for me was a weekly outdoor column in our local paper. Outdoor stores often maintain a chalkboard with local waters and the current conditions and suggestions for tackle. Your local fly club can be a great source of tips and current information.

The internet is now a prolific source of information, some of it accurate. For those unlucky streams saddled with dams there is often real-time data on stream flows. Fly shops host web pages that often include current information about local streams and lakes.

Another source is the people you meet streamside. The local convenience store: Of course you need a cup of coffee; stop in and be friendly and see what they know. Separate the wheat from the chaff. Local vendors have a vested interest in attracting anglers, so they may be wearing "rose-colored glasses."

If other anglers are on stream, wait until they take a break and then step up and be friendly. Golden Rule of Human Nature: If they have done well they will tell you all about it.

I find that most people stream-side or lake-side are friendly and helpful. Approach them in a friendly and respectful manner and they will usually reciprocate.

One evening years ago, I fished Merrill Lake, a fly-only lake in Western Washington. I fished energetically from my car-top boat for several hours that summer evening and was rewarded with two decent brown trout. Walking ashore in the fading sunset, I spotted a couple sitting in lawn-chairs. Friendly and relaxed together, they seemed the epitome of middle-aged contentment. We chatted. They asked how I had done; I related the fish I caught and the flies I had used. I asked them how they had done. They had caught 40 trout between them.

Forty trout! Wow! What did you catch them on? The husband extended the fly to me for inspection: a small, nondescript nymph, perhaps a #14 pheasant-tail or similar fly. Where did you catch them? They pointed to the shore just a few yards away. The

shoreline formed a small cove no more than thirty yards in diameter. Wow, right there from shore? Yes, indeed. As I walked away, I turned and asked: What size were they? The husband grinned as he held up his thumb and index finger spanning all of three inches– "everyone was about this big."

To get the right answers, you must ask the right questions.

Learn the "rules," then learn when to throw them away

In this respect fly fishing is no different than learning to write an essay. First you learn the rules of grammar, punctuation, and syntax. Then you learn there are some alternative usages and grey areas. Then, reading Ernest Hemingway or James Joyce, you observe that they flat-out break the rules. But they break the rules only after thoroughly understanding the rules and the reasons for ignoring them.

Don't be afraid to fail

Continually experiment until you find what works. I often talk to anglers streamside who have fished a bit, tried this or that and are standing around and seemed to have given up. I've done it myself. Keep experimenting: Try a different drift, a different water type, a sinking line, a different fly type.

The river has a story to tell; we must learn to listen

Honing your powers of observation is one of the great benefits of fly fishing. We seem to approach nature with preconceived ideas and desires; we look for what we want to see or expect to see.

It's hard. We humans seem programmed to talk rather than listen. In the book of I Samuel, Samuel says "Speak Lord, your servant is listening." We humans tend to say, "Listen, Lord, your servant is speaking."

Years ago, I visited Lucia Falls on the Lewis River in Southwest Washington. I did not go to fish–this section of the river is and was closed to all angling.

The winter rains and snowfalls had filled hundreds of creeks that became tributaries that became the main river and now funneled through a narrow opening in the rocks at the top of the falls. About 200 cubic feet of water per second burst through the opening and plunged 15 feet into the circular pool below.

It was a bright, late-summer morning. Carefully, with nervous glances into the ice-cold churning depths below me, I climbed over moss-covered rocks damp with the spray from the falls to reach a vantage point looking directly down into the pool.

Suddenly, out of the depths an eight-pound, summer-run steelhead leaped violently into the air, struggled against the falling water, then fell back into the pool. Then another and another leaped, but each fell back. The casual observer might conclude that this was the end of the line for these fish, that the falls stopped their upward migration, but this is not true. Later, a steelhead leaped against the falls and swam up and up and finally swam over the top and disappeared into the pool above the falls. Fish leaping a waterfall don't make a single leap and clear the falls like a high-jumper clearing the bar. They leap into the falls, then swim up near-vertically until they clear the top. The initial leap takes them perhaps halfway over.

Eventually these fish would clear the falls and push on to upstream spawning grounds. Many would wait until the fall and winter rains filled the pool thus lowering the height of the falls.

The fish stopped jumping. I stared into the depths of the pool. Occasionally I would catch a glimpse of a steelhead deep in the pool ghosting between rock ledges deep in the pool.

For how many years had these fish been leaping this waterfall? The river hosted runs of both wild and hatchery fish. The summer runs were mainly hatchery fish from the nearby Skamania hatchery. But there was also a wild run of steelhead that returned April to June but did not spawn until the following early spring, the "springer" run of steelhead that also ran up the Washougal and Kalama rivers.

Perhaps a few of these fish were wild, springer steelhead. If so, their ancestors must have been leaping these falls a hundred years ago, when the first loggers began working the surrounding forests. The fish returned here each spring when the Native American tribes met and traded goods and gambled at Moulton Falls upstream a few miles; long before The Lewis and Clark Expedition camped on the Columbia River some twenty miles to the south. Long before the first Native American tribes settled nearby, the fish were jumping these falls. Perhaps before the Missoula Floods scoured the land 17,000 years ago. Long before that, perhaps back to when the Cascade Mountains slowly rose above the plain. Floods, volcanoes, forest fires, and drought might have temporarily wiped out the run, but, aided by stray fish from neighboring rivers, the run would rebuild.

How many springs had seen these fish return? Many more than we can imagine. They are the stars of the show. We are just bit-players, at best.

18. Angling Etiquette, Sportsmanship, and Conservation

Part 2 of this book explained the basic skills needed to enjoy fly fishing. Most introductory fly fishing books today stop at that point. That's a huge mistake. The sport of fly fishing does not maintain itself by some magical force; it has been maintained and developed, over decades and centuries, by people who care about the sport and desire that it thrive for their children and grandchildren.

The Fly Fishers International (FFI) is devoted to conservation, education, and community to ensure the legacy and further the sport of fly fishing. The FFI has developed its *Code of Angling Ethics*, which I have included in this volume as Appendix 2. Throughout this chapter I have included short excerpts from the FFI *Code* in bold italic type, followed by my own commentary, which reflects my own thoughts and does not necessarily reflect the views of the FFI, though I hope it does.

> ***"Fly anglers treat fellow anglers as they would expect to be treated."***

> ***"Fly anglers when sharing the water allow fellow anglers ample room so as to not disturb anyone's fishing experience."***

Respect for and Fair Treatment of Fellow Anglers

If you always find yourself alone when fishing, just skip this section. What ??.... Other anglers share the water with you where you fish?? Surprise, surprise! Today, it is the rare angler that finds himself fishing alone or with a few chosen companions. For all of us to be able to enjoy the sport in an atmosphere of respect and harmony, we need to adhere to and promote a code of conduct on the water.

The basic rule of courtesy has been described as the "Golden Rule": Do unto others as you would have them do unto you. The only problem with this is it *assumes you have knowledge of what the other person needs from you.* Beginning fly anglers don't always understand the need to allow the other angler plenty of space and the ability to work through a stretch of water without being cut off.

So, even if you are fully committed to being thoughtful and courteous, you need to read through this next section and understand what other anglers need.

Crowded situations often arise because of concentrations of hatchery fish at a given place and time. These can be either returning anadromous fish or recently stocked trout on a lake. Either situation can attract an army of folks wielding both fly and spin rods.

Don't crowd other anglers. If you approach a drift or pool and another angler is there already, ask if you can join him or her. Also, observe or ask if they are moving upstream or down, and if you join them, join *behind* them. This is the unwritten rule of "the line forms at the rear." This is a rule that beginners may not immediately understand. One reason is that the angler or anglers in place may be moving downstream slowly, so if you don't watch for a few minutes you may think that they are stationary and it would be just fine to pop in between two of them. Wait and watch a few minutes or ask first.

The above "line forms at the rear" rule is an example of the "when in Rome do as the Romans" concept: In areas where anglers tend to concentrate, local anglers often develop protocols, or "rules of the road," that presumably work well in the local situation. So, you are advised to ask, watch, and fit in.

On lakes, observe the "two-cast rule": Try to maintain a distance between boats at least equal to two long casts. If you are in a boat and there are people fishing from shore, give them wide berth. You can fish the entire lake and they cannot.

We are all different, in temperament, personality, and communication style. You and your fishing pals might be having a great time drinking beer and swapping yarns, in a boisterous, hearty manner, but others around you may have come to the river to experience solitude and quiet, and they may not appreciate your behavior. There is room for give or take. Just be aware and considerate.

"Fly anglers do not judge the methods of fellow anglers."

Elitism and other Fishing Methods

Some folks seem to think that being a fly fisher makes you superior to those folks who resort to bait or lure fishing. I disagree.

In 19th century England, only the aristocrats had the means and opportunity to fly fish for trout and Atlantic salmon. The working-class blokes had to be content to enjoy "rough fish." They, for their part, developed artistic and sporting methods for catching these fish.

Fly fishing, one would hope, has shaken off the tentacles of its aristocratic roots. I believe it has. Tennis and golf also grew out of distinctly upper-class, country-club roots, but today these sports are enjoyed by people of all ages, races, and socioeconomic backgrounds.

Elitism within fly fishing

On a hot August day years ago, I fished the Deschutes River for trout. By mid-afternoon I had caught nothing. Two brothers were fishing nearby, and they invited me to share a beer in the shade with them. We talked and enjoyed the cold beer and the shade. Their luck had been as bad as mine. They had to return home, so I thanked them for their hospitality, then decided to fish one more time before the two-hour drive home. I hiked upstream a few hundred yards to a large, broad riffle, tied on a #6, weighted stonefly nymph, and began to drift it deeply through the riffle. In a few minutes, I was rewarded by a solid strike and a good fight. Shortly, a fine, 14-inch, "redside" rainbow was in hand and released. Some minutes later, another redside, this one slightly smaller but brighter, grabbed the big nymph, fought well, and also was released. I was preparing for the drive home when a young man stopped by to talk.

"What were you wrangling with up there?" he asked. It seemed a strange question.

"Two nice rainbows; fourteen and twelve inches." I replied.

"What did you catch them with?" he asked haughtily.

"A weighted stonefly nymph, fished down deep."

"Oh.... well...., I guess you can catch them anytime, if you are willing to go deep."

Ugh. What happened to "Nice trout! Thanks for the tip about the weighted stonefly."

The above encounter demonstrates a prevalent elitism based on "superior" fly fishing method. Sure, you caught a fish but "I only fish dry, you know......."; "I only fish greased line for steelhead, you know...."

In England at the turn of the 20th century, on many streams, fishing an upstream dry fly to a rising trout was the only method allowed. An English lawyer, G.E.M. Skues, developed techniques for fishing realistic nymph patterns upstream, dead-drift. For his efforts Skues found himself *banned* from many streams. *Banned!* Not for poaching fish, not for drunkenness, not for harassing the young kitchen maids, but for fishing with a method deemed to be "inferior." Skues went on to publish several excellent books explaining his techniques, and is now considered the father of modern nymph fishing.

There is nothing wrong with preferring one fly fishing method to others. It's natural to do so. There is nothing wrong with recommending your methods to others. There is nothing wrong with concluding that certain methods simply aren't for you. For my sins, a soft-hackle fly fished right below the surface with a floating line cannot be beat. But when one goes from holding a strong preference, to believing that your preferred method is *superior,* and other methods are thus by default *inferior*, you have crossed the line to elitism.

Fly anglers are sometimes accused of being elitist snobs sporting tweed jackets and sipping chilled chardonnay served stream-side by their man-servants. Hopefully it's an image that's rarely deserved.

The Highest and Best Use Concept

"Highest and best use" is a legal or land valuation term I have borrowed to refer to a second principle that might be viewed as contradicting the no-elitism principle above.

This second sportsmanship concept has been around for a long time in both hunting and fishing and could be stated as follows: A true sportsman strives to utilize the most sporting and challenging method that makes sense under the circumstances and the quarry at hand. By sporting method is meant the method that will give the angler or hunter the most satisfaction per animal caught or killed, and still have a reasonable chance of success. It implies a hierarchy of methods for any situation. It implies refraining from certain methods because they are, in the situation in question, too easy, therefore not sportsmanlike.

Roderick Haig-Brown, dean of Pacific Northwest angling authors, went as far as to outline a hierarchy of methods for each of his favorite fish, such as summer-run steelhead, sea-run cutthroat, etc. (*Western Angler*, Part V, Chapter 3). For each he listed methods from most preferred to least preferred. He also states that he finds none of the methods unattractive and he was prepared to use any provided the method would do no harm and that there was no chance of success using the methods above it. Here is his hierarchy for the steelhead:

1. Greased line
2. Deep-sunk fly
3. Wet fly
4. Dry fly
5. Devon prawn
6. Prawn
7. Spoon or spinner
8. Fly with spinner
9. Spinner with bait

And then he concluded by saying "if it looks as if I shall have to go down below No. 3 or 4 on any list, I am likely enough to seize an opportunity to be virtuous and stay at home to get some work done."

I do not believe this second principle contradicts the no-elitism principle, rather it stands in a state of tension to it. The secret to observing both ethical principles revolves around **attitude and communication.**

Let's say it's a fine summer day. You are working your way up a small mountain stream, tossing bushy dry flies into the pockets and heads of pools. You have caught and released five or six 10-inch rainbows and cutthroats and hooked others. Around a bend, you meet up with a couple of young fellows catching and creeling similar fish by bouncing night crawlers along the bottom below a bobber (perfectly legal on this stream). Be friendly, helpful, and non-judgmental. As you are chatting with them you might show them your flies and indicate that they are effective on these fish (and lots of fun). Even give them a few and show them how to fish them below the bobbers they are already using. You may win converts and perhaps friends.

"Fly anglers respect private property and always ask permission before entering or fishing private property."

Respect for the Rights of Property Owners and other Stream Users

"No Trespassing" signs blocking our way to streams and lakes. We curse the property owner, but is there really any wonder that he has posted his property when you consider the piles of trash and the late-night revelry he must endure? In England, the streams are privately owned, and if you care to fish them you must pay the owner a handsome fee to rent a "beat," or section of river, for a specified number of hours. Pay to play.

We anglers need to respect private property rights and work with landowners to increase access. It is a two-way street.

Picture a sunny, July Saturday; you drive for an hour, then hike for another hour to a favorite secluded spot on a stream. Sweating and huffing but filled with anticipation of great fishing, you arrive at your secret spot. As you rig your fly rod you hear splashing and children laughing. Sprinting down to the riverside you find that "your" secret spot has been commandeered by a family with lawn chairs; the young kids playing in the water and the older boys are jumping off rocks into the depths of the pool.

Sure, you are disappointed, ...but mad? ...... At whom? They have just as much right to use the stream as you do. So, what to do? You skulk around them ......try to hurry them up....... adopt a pouting attitude. You are reinforcing the stereotype of the elitist fly fisherman. No, instead, be friendly and chat with them. The kids will tire of the swimming and be heading home and you will probably get the pool to yourself for the evening.

"Angling ethics begin with understanding and obeying laws and regulations associated with the fishery."

A baseline for sportsmanship is following the local fishing regulations ("regs") in force in your state. These regs are developed by your state fish and game department and ultimately made law by your state legislature. Thus, the regs are "political" and will not satisfy everyone. Often anglers complain about the complexity of the laws, but the laws have as their goal the protection of the fisheries balanced by the goal of making the resource available for harvest. Various interest groups–commercial fisheries, sport fishing groups, environmental groups–all joust for position and the laws are the result of the political process.

It's amazing that the regs are as good as they are considering the competing interest groups at play. Sport fishing groups themselves often take diametrically opposed views on an issue, with one group pushing for expanded harvest and another arguing for catch and release and other protections. Tourist industry lobbyists strong-arm politicians to push for expanded catch and kill limits.

Regardless of the complexity of the regs, it is absolutely essential that anglers read and understand the regs for the waters they intend to fish.

I find it instructive to read through the regs and look for waters designated as one or more of the following:

- Catch and release
- Restrictive gear
- Fly only

Often these waters are ones that the game department is trying to develop into a "quality fishery." If you plan on practicing catch and release, you have a huge advantage over your catch-and-eat fishing friends in that you can fish the restrictive gear and catch and release waters.

"Fly anglers endeavor to conserve fisheries by understanding the importance of limiting their catch."

Protection and Enhancement of the Resource

To catch a fish there must be fish in the water. This basic truism seems to elude certain folks. For fish to thrive, there must be clean water, adequate spawning grounds, and plentiful organisms for the fish to eat. In a word, a healthy ecosystem. If for no other reason than unrefined self-interest, anglers should do whatever they can to protect and enhance fisheries eco-systems.

Catch and Release

Over the thirty-five years I have been fly fishing, I have witnessed the widespread acceptance and adoption of catch and release fishing. I personally release all but one or two hatchery fish per season, usually a trout to throw on the coals while camping. It is really a no-brainer when you give it some thought. Do you really want to drag around a couple of trout in your backpack all afternoon, scramble to the store to buy ice, get home late in the evening, then fry up the trout? Do they really taste that great? Or is it a matter of proving your manly prowess to folks back home? I found the transition to catch and release an easy one. If folks would objectively compare the costs of store-bought fish to the costs of their fishing trips they would conclude that sport-fishing with the goal of saving money on groceries, in this day and age, is a hopeless cause.

Making Catch and Release Effective: Barbless Hooks, Fly-only Waters, and Restrictive Regs

Regulations that limit catch, either size restrictions or an outright no-kill rule, are of no value if the fish does not survive after release. There is a serious problem with bait fishing on rivers and lakes where some or all fish are legally required to be released. Since the bait tastes and smells real, the fish tends to take the bait deep into its mouth thus causing internal damage and, when released, often fails to survive. Most trout waters have a minimum size for retaining fish, so this problem applies not only to catch and release waters but to virtually all waters holding wild trout, because, due to normal predation, a stream will usually hold more small fish than larger ones. With lures and flies, the fish does not allow the bogus intrusion to get far into its mouth; it either expels it or is hooked in the lip or outer jaw making quick release easier.

Barbless hooks aid in the successful release of trout by easing the process of removing the hook therefore reducing the time the fish is out of water. I have been using barbless hooks exclusively for at least 20 years and have no regrets. The biggest advantage is the ease with which I can release fish. Barbless hooks are mandatory on many waters to facilitate the quick and non-lethal release of fish as required.

Fly-only regs have been established on limited waters in many states. The purposes of such regs are twofold: conservation purposes and "social" purposes.

Conservation reasons are as stated above, to increase post-release survival, and to limit harvest in general. A general limiting of harvest occurs because fly fishing is considered a less aggressive method than others. Fly fishing, though effective for trout, will be effective fewer days during a given season than, for example, bait fishing.

By "social" reasons for fly–only waters, I mean that fly anglers need more room to cast and thus a greater spacing between participants. Fly anglers, due to their more limited casting range, tend to move constantly while fishing, however lure and bait anglers often stay put for longer periods of time. The intent is to avoid conflicts and allow both groups to fish in harmony.

For these reasons, a very limited number of waters, or just portions of streams, have been designated fly-only. Yet, despite fly-only water extending to less than 1 percent of all fishable water, loud cries of elitism are heard.

As an alternative to fly-only waters, Washington and many other states also use **Selective Gear Rules** for certain waters. The main idea here is to ban bait and require barbless hooks on those waters hosting wild fish.

The following is from the state of Washington fishing regulations guide:

Selective Gear Rules:

Only unscented artificial flies or lures with one single-point, barbless hook are allowed. Up to a total of three artificial flies or lures, each containing one single-point, barbless hook may be used. Bait is prohibited; fish may be released until the daily limit is retained. Only knotless nets may be used to land fish except where specifically allowed under Special Rules for individual waters. If any fish has swallowed the hook or is hooked in the gill, eye, or tongue, it should be kept if legal to do so.

An excellent way to help enhance and protect fisheries is to become active in a fly fishing organization. Most are involved in efforts to protect fisheries, both through boots on the ground conservation projects, streamside cleanups, and the like, and political involvement. Both are important. The former gives the volunteers an immediate gratification in terms of a cleaned-up boat launch, newly planted streamside trees, or the like. Tangible results followed by refreshments around a campfire or at a local tavern. Political involvement most likely won't yield these pleasures. Sending letters, attending acrimonious late-night meetings, encountering opposition at the grocery store; these are, for most of us, not fun. But it is important work and local clubs often develop the contacts and skills to be effective in the political arena. Power dam licensing, dam removal, mining and timber harvest, environmental protections or the lack thereof, restrictive fishing regs to build wild fish populations: I would bet that in your communities these issues are brewing in the political arena, and the future of our fisheries hangs in the balance.

Teaching the next generation: a Clark-Skamania Fly Fishers casting clinic. Photo by John Geyer.

Joining a local club can also be a great source of assistance for the rookie fly fisher. Most clubs are happy to help beginners and may conduct casting clinics and outings appropriate for their skill level. I say, can be, not will be, for unfortunately not all clubs and not all club members are open and helpful to beginners. If you attend a few meetings and find the members cliquish or snobbish, and you honestly feel you have given it a fair shot, then move on and try a different club or organization.

19. Angling Traditions

No one knows exactly when fly fishing began. The earliest written record of fly fishing seems to be *A Treatyse on Fysshynge wyth an Angle,* published in 1496 and attributed to Dame Juliana Berners, a nun and prioress of the Order of St Benedict.

There is no room in this present work to survey the entire 500-year history of fly fishing. My purpose here is to give the reader a taste of that history and perhaps engender his or her interest in learning about the anglers who helped develop the sport.

One way to deepen your enjoyment of the sport is to dip into the fine body of books written about fly fishing. You will begin to appreciate that the sport grows out of traditions: shared understandings, experiences, and opinions that are refined and passed on from one generation to the next. By reading you will see that anglers from earlier generations shared with you similar hopes, frustrations, and joys.

Traditions start when anglers discover a promising fishery, fish it and learn its secrets, then meet other like-minded anglers and share flies, techniques, stories, etc. They get to know each other, as a group of "regulars." Then time passes, old regulars die, young ones join and hear stories of the earlier anglers, books may be written, a "second-generation" takes the helm, passing on stories and flies developed by the first generation. Techniques and flies are refined and debated around campfires and tavern fireplaces. Eventually a tradition is passed on to future generations.

Traditions are also enshrined in fly patterns. Behind a pattern is often a story, and often includes the man or woman who designed the fly, the waters it was first used on, and possibly a culture of anglers that the designer fished with.

I would encourage you to learn about fly fishing traditions in the areas you fish. Below is a thumbnail sketch of one important tradition from our beautiful Pacific Northwest.

The North Fork of the Stillaguamish River

From its source about fifteen miles north of the town of Darrington, Washington, the North Fork "Stilly" first flows south, then, joined by Squire Creek, flows westward for nearly 45 miles to join the South Fork near the town of Arlington. Along these 45 miles it passes through gentle farming land dotted with tiny hamlets. All in the shadow of Glacier Peak.

At the town of Oso it is joined by Deer Creek, its largest tributary and one of great importance to this story. Deer Creek hosted (and still hosts in, sadly, much-reduced numbers) one of the greatest runs of summer steelhead to be found anywhere in the world. The fish are a breed apart, small by steelhead standards, averaging four or five pounds, bullet-shaped and bright silver upon arrival in June, they are highly responsive to flies, even to surface flies.

In 1918, Zane Grey, the brash author of outdoor and adventure books, fished the North Fork at Deer Creek and there caught his first steelhead. This is thought to be the first steelhead caught by a white settler on the North Fork. Grey recounted the event in his *Tales of Freshwater Fishing*, 1928:

> *Deer Creek was the most beautiful trout water I had ever seen. Clear as crystal, cold as ice, it spoke eloquently of the pure springs of the mountain fastness. Under the water the rocks were amber-colored, and along the banks they were green with moss and gray with lichen.*

Grey goes on to recount he and his companions catching beautiful steelhead using bait, not flies.

Some 10 years later Roderick Haig-Brown hiked into Deer Creek in pursuit of its fabled summer steelhead. On his initial hike to Deer Creek, he caught fish, but doubted they were steelhead. He was right; he was to learn later that they were Dolly Varden. A few weeks later he returned and this time landed a seven-pound, bright, Deer Creek steelhead, his first steelhead. He caught it, and the Dolly Vardens, on lures, not flies.

Over the next decade, roads were laid and settlers increased. More and more anglers began to fish the North Fork and Deer Creek. Catching steelhead on a fly ceased to be considered a fabulous pipe dream and became a recognized technique, at least for the summer runs.

In 1935 a group of fly anglers, led by Enos Bradner, a Seattle bookstore owner who later became outdoor writer for the Seattle Times, petitioned the state of Washington to designate the North Fork Stillaguamish as a fly fishing only river. The restrictions were to be in effect only from May through November each year. Winter steelhead could be caught using any legal method. This was to be the first river or lake in Washington state to be so designated.

All hell broke loose. Local opposition deemed it elitist. Meetings were held and tempers flared. Many testifying against the proposed regulations had never once fished the river. The state Game Commission first accepted, then rejected the proposal, then finally, due to the tenacity of Bradner and other members of the newly formed Washington Fly Fishing Club, the commission declared the North Fork, from May through November of each year, a fly fishing only river.

With the fly fishing only regulations in force, from 1944 until the 1980s the river entered what might be called its Golden Age. A group of "regulars" formed that included experts from throughout the Pacific Northwest. Tackle and techniques, such as shooting heads, sink-tip lines, and stripping-baskets, were developed. Flies were designed: Stillaguamish Sunrise, Brad's Brat, Purple Peril, and scores of others were developed and refined along the banks of the river. Books were written that included chapters lovingly reflecting on the river and its amazing fish. The Stilly's sea-run cutthroats, though often playing second fiddle to the steelhead, developed ardent followers.

Indiscriminate logging destroyed this paradise. In the 1960s and '70s most of the Deer Creek watershed was logged. The soil in this region, for reasons beyond my understanding, is prone to slides. The now-bare slopes, fueled by winter rainstorms, shed their soil in a muddy torrent that turned the water the color of cement and silted the main stem Stilly for miles below the mouth of Deer Creek.

The Deer Creek steelhead run plummeted. In the mid-1990s the run had dropped to a few dozen returning adults. Hatchery fish were first planted in the Stilly in 1960 and by this time provided most of the fishing. The hatchery fish ran upriver to the "Fortson Hole" where the state fish and game department maintained rearing ponds for the juvenile fish. Most of the fishing concentrated at this point during the fall months when the adults congregated here. Gone was most of the summer fishing along the length of the river and at the mouth of Deer Creek, called the "Elbow Hole" by regulars.

Now efforts to revive the Deer Creek run continue. Most of the "old timers"–Enos Bradner, Wes Drain, Al Knudsen, Ralph Wahl, Ken McLeod and his son George, my own father Bill Green–have passed away. Now a new generation of anglers strives to rebuild the fishery and carry forward the traditions nurtured along the banks of this beautiful stream.

Brad's Brat

Enos Bradner of Seattle devised this pattern in 1937 for steelhead and sea-run cutthroat on his beloved "Stilly." It has remained a standard throughout the Pacific Northwest for the last 70-some years.

Bradner was born in Michigan, graduated from the University of Michigan, then served in the US Army in World War I in France. In 1929 he traveled to Washington state and fell in love with the area and its rivers. He moved to Seattle and bought a bookstore.

Bradner became a legend in Pacific Northwest fishing circles. He was instrumental in gaining the fly only restrictions on the North Fork in 1944. His book, *Northwest Angling*, published in 1950, has become a standard text for Washington fly anglers. He bought a cabin on the banks of the North Fork at the mouth of Deer Creek near to town of Oso and spent many days in pursuit of the river's beloved summer-run steelhead.

Brad's Brat is an example of a pattern that can be tied in various sizes in order to target different runs of fish. Tied on size #4 to #6 hooks for summer-run steelhead, #4 to 2/0 for winter steelhead, and #6 to #10 for sea-run cutthroat.

Tag: Gold tinsel

Tail: Orange and white bucktail

Body: Rear half orange wool; front half red wool

Rib: Flat gold tinsel

Hackle: Brown

Wing: Orange over white bucktail

Cheek: Jungle Cock - optional

20. For Further Reading

We read in order to understand that we are not alone.
C.S. Lewis in the film *Shadowlands*.

Fly fishing literature encompasses many genres. Some are how-to-do-it books like the one you are reading; some are specialized studies on a single subject, such as caddisflies, steelhead fishing, or brown trout; others are where-to-go books, guides to fishing a certain river or region; another group are more like memoirs, reflective and philosophical, asking "Why do I do this crazy thing called fly fishing?"

When I first got the "fly fishing bug" at age 27, I searched for books to help me learn the craft. Of all the books I read, *Curtis Creek Manifesto,* listed below, provided the most practical help. But I also discovered the writings of Roderick Haig-Brown. I was captivated by the beautiful writing style and the beauty of the places and fishing he described. I set a dream for myself to follow his lead and write a book of my own. Now, 35 years later, I have realized that dream. Haig-Brown was and is, the inspiration for this book.

Roderick Haig-Brown, 1908-1976, Canadian author, justice of the peace, and Chancellor of the University of Victoria

Born in Sussex, England, before World War I, Roderick grew up on the banks of the Fromm River. His father was killed in action in France in 1918. A family friend, Major Greenhill, took over the boy's outdoor education, taught him to cast a fly, to work a lure for salmon, and to hunt birds. Young Roderick excelled at all. His inquiring mind absorbed the lessons and he became a keen observer of nature. As a young man, he immigrated to British Columbia and Washington state and worked as a logger. Here he applied the classical English fly fishing training of his boyhood to the brawling, uncharted waters of the Pacific Northwest and expressed his knowledge in a series of fly fishing books unparalleled in their clarity of thought, beauty of language, and calm mastery of subject matter.

In 1934 he married Ann Elmore of Seattle, and they settled on a farm on the banks of the Campbell River on Vancouver Island. Here he would spend the next 40 years: raising a family, farming, fly fishing, and writing. *The Western Angler, A River Never Sleeps, Return to the River, A Fisherman's Spring, A Fisherman's Fall,* these and others established him as one of the greatest fly fishing writers of all time.

His classic upstream dry fly fishing on gentle English streams he kept and applied when it made sense, but developed bushy dry flies and radical techniques that caught fish in the rough-and-tumble rivers of the Pacific Northwest. He developed and refined wet fly techniques for the migratory steelhead and cutthroat trout. In everything he kept the old and adapted to the new.

He broke down long-standing myths about what you could, or more pointedly couldn't, catch with a fly or with a dry fly. He wrote that when he first moved to the Northwest "accounts of catching steelhead on a fly were considered no better than wild tales." The only thing that would work, so he was solemnly instructed, was fresh salmon roe liberally draped onto a large hook and bounced along the stream bottom. Ignoring this advice, he caught summer steelhead on lures, wet flies, then on dry flies, and finally, winter steelhead on deeply-sunk wet flies.

Haig-Brown did not develop these techniques alone but in collaboration with other anglers, both Canadian and American: General Noel Money, the artist Tommy Brayshaw, the photographer Ralph Wahl, innovative rod builder Letcher Lambuth, to name a few.

GENERAL WORKS

Anderson, Sheridan. *Curtis Creek Manifesto*. Portland, Oregon; Frank Amato Publications, 1973.
> *Formatted as a comic book with more illustrations than text, this classic work is an easy to understand, humorous, yet sound and complete introduction to fly fishing.*

Gierach, John. *Trout Bum*. New York; Simon and Schuster Paperbacks, 1986.
> *Gierach can tell a story. And he is a trout bum that knows his stuff. You will have trouble putting this book down.*

Haig-Brown, Roderick. *A River Never Sleeps*. Winchester, Ontario; Winchester Press, 1974.
> *By one of the all-time great angling writers. Describes month-by-month the delights of nature and angling, weaving scenes from his boyhood England in with his adopted Canadian steelhead streams and trout lakes.*

Haig-Brown, Roderick. *A Primer on Fly Fishing*. New York; William and Morrow Co., 1964.
> *This classic work explains fly lines, leaders, casting, wading, reading water, fly selection, as well as conservation and ethics. Still timely, though written some fifty years ago.*

Hemingway, Ernest. *Big Two-Hearted River (Part I and Part II)*, from *The Complete Short Stories of Ernest Hemingway*. New York; Simon & Schuster, 1987.
> *Every fly fisher should read this short story by the master of the unstated. Nick Adam returns from war injured in body and spirit. To recuperate, he embarks on a solo hiking and fishing trip. Adams does not fly fish on this journey – he uses a fly rod and line to cast live grasshoppers – but the "big-hearted" spirit shines through.*

Hemingway, Ernest. *The Old Man and the Sea*. New York; Charles Scribner's Sons, 1952.
> *Once you have been bitten by the fishing bug, you may see something of yourself in the aging Santiago and his epic struggle with a huge Marlin. Note the reverence that Santiago begins to feel for the huge fish, as hours of struggle turn into days.*

Raymond, Steve. *The Year of the Angler*. Seattle, Washington; Sasquatch Books, 1995.
> *With evocative prose, this well-known Seattle journalist and writer guides us on a tour of his beloved trout streams and lakes of the Pacific Northwest.*

Schwiebert, Ernest. *Death of a Riverkeeper*. San Francisco; Donald S. Ellis., 1984.
> *This collection recounts the author's fishing adventures from Montana to Iceland to Oregon to the Florida Keys. Schwiebert is a master of both the fly rod and the written word. Always interesting, sometimes humorous, sometimes deeply moving.*

CASTING

Kreh, Lefty. *Fly Casting Fundamentals.* **Mechanicsburg, Pennsylvania; Stackpole Books, 2012.**

Both casting basics and a multitude of advanced casting techniques are demonstrated via hundreds of photographs and clear text. I wish I could perform half of the casts in this book. Maybe someday. An excellent teaching tool.

TROUT BIOLOGY AND CONSERVATION

Brown, Bruce. *Mountain in the Clouds.* **New York; Simon and Schuster, 1982.**

The author hiked and boated throughout the Olympic Peninsula seeking to understand its wild salmon and trout. He studied the history of settlement and industrial development in the region. The magnitude of the demise of these magnificent fish stared him in the face. The culprits: individual and corporate greed aided by government agencies that gamboled between bumbling incompetence and steely-eyed, determined complicity. But the story has a few heroes, men and women who, like the salmon, swam against the flow and labored to save these beautiful fish.

Smith, Robert H. *Native Trout of North America.* **Portland, Oregon; Frank Amato Publications, 1984.**

One day Bob Smith caught a hatchery trout in a beautiful stream in which he had hoped to catch a wild trout. The trout was fin-clipped, about a foot long, and obviously raised in concrete tanks and fed pellets. Smith had an epiphany. He rebelled. He launched on a personal journey to catch, record, study, and revere wild, native trout. His journey took him throughout North America to tiny creeks holding remnant populations of native cutthroats and rainbows. Very readable and inspiring.

Trotter, Patrick C. *Cutthroat, Native Trout of the West.* **Boulder, Colorado; Colorado Associated University Press, 1987.**

Painstakingly researched yet fully accessible to the non-scientist reader. The many subspecies of the cutthroat trout, their evolution, their historical range, and status are detailed via maps and text.

Willers, Bill. *Trout Biology; A Natural History of Trout and Salmon.* **New York; Lyons and Burford, 1991.**

The angler's basic bible on trout biology. Well-written and informative; completely readable by the non-technical reader. My copy is underlined, highlighted, and worn out.

THE FOODS TROUT EAT

Hafele, Rick and Hughes, Dave. *The Complete Book of Western Hatches*. **Portland, Oregon; Frank Amato Publications, 1981.**

Each major insect group is explained in non-technical language with plentiful photographs, diagrams and line drawings. Recommended patterns and their presentations are offered. I carry mine streamside and lakeside and refer to it often.

PRESENTATION

Scott, Jock. *Greased Line Fishing for Salmon*. **Portland, Oregon; Frank Amato Publications, 1982.**

Based on the "fishing papers" of Arthur Wood of Scotland, this remarkable book describes a theory of fishing for salmon that involves a floating line and small flies fished with little or no drag right below the surface of the stream. Mending is the secret to this technique. Also applicable to trout fishing.

Sylvester Nemes. *The Soft- Hackled Fly*. **Old Greenwich, Connecticut; The Chatham Press, 1975.**

Soft-hackled flies are some of the oldest flies and perhaps the simplest. The author describes fishing with these flies on rivers in his native Michigan as well as those in Colorado and Montana. His techniques rely heavily on mending and line control. Well-written, informative and enjoyable.

Appendices

Appendix 1- A Simplified Taxonomy of the Salmonids

FAMILY: Salmonidae
  SUB-FAMILY Salmoninae
    GENUS: *Oncorynchus*

SPECIES:	*Oncorynchus mykiss*	**Rainbow trout**
	O. clarkii	**Cutthroat trout**
	O. kisutch	**Silver (coho) salmon**
	O. tshawytscha	**King (chinook) salmon**
	O. keta	**Chum (dog) salmon**
	O. gorbuscha	**Humpback (pink) salmon**
	O. nerka	**Sockeye (red) salmon**
	O. masou	**Cherry salmon**
	O. apache	**Apache trout**
	O. chrysogaster	**Mexican golden trout**
	O. gilae	**Gila trout**
	O. kawamurae	**Black kokanee**

    GENUS: *Salmo*

SPECIES:	*Salmo salar*	**Atlantic salmon**
	Salmo trutta	**Brown trout**

(As many as 48 additional species not in this book)

    GENUS: *Salvelinus*

SPECIES:	*Salvelinus fontinalis*	**Brook trout**
	S. malma	**Dolly Varden**
	S. confluentus	**Bull trout**

(As many as 49 additional species not in this book)

    GENUS:
(Four additional genera, not referred to in this book, are recognized: *Brachymystax, Hucho, Parahucho, and Salvethymus*)

Appendix 2 – Fly Fishers International *Code of Angling Ethics*

- Angling ethics begin with understanding and obeying laws and regulations associated with the fishery. Fly anglers understand that their conduct relative to laws and regulations reflects on all anglers. Angling ethics begin with and transcend laws and regulations governing angling and the resources that sustain the sport.

- The opportunity to participate in the sport of fly fishing is a privilege and a responsibility. Fly anglers respect private property and always ask permission before entering or fishing private property. They seek to understand and follow the local customs and practices associated with the fishery. They share the waters equally with others whether they are fishing or engaging in other outdoor activities.

- Fly fishers minimize their impact on the environment and fishery by adopting practices that do not degrade the quality of the banks, waters, and the overall watersheds upon which fisheries depend. These practices include avoiding the introduction of species not native to an ecosystem, and cleaning and drying fishing gear to prevent the inadvertent transport of invasive exotics that may threaten the integrity of an aquatic ecosystem. In simplest terms, fly anglers always leave the fishery better than when they found it.

- Fly anglers endeavor to conserve fisheries by understanding the importance of limiting their catch. "Catch and release" is an important component of sustaining premium fisheries that are being over-harvested. Fly anglers release fish properly and with minimal harm. They promote the use of barbless hooks and angling practices that are more challenging but which help to sustain healthy fish populations.

- Fly anglers do not judge the methods of fellow anglers. Fly fishers share their knowledge of skills and techniques. They help others to understand that fly fishing contributes to sound fisheries conservation practices.

- Fly anglers treat fellow anglers as they would expect to be treated. They do not impose themselves on or otherwise interfere with other anglers. They wait a polite time, and then, if necessary, request permission to fish through. They may invite other anglers to fish through their positions. Fly fishers when entering an occupied run or area always move in behind other anglers, not in front of them whether in a boat or wading.

- Fly anglers when sharing the water allow fellow anglers ample room so as not to disturb anyone's fishing experience. They always fish in a manner that causes as little disturbance as practical to the water and fish. They take precautions to keep their shadow from falling across the water (walking a high bank).

- When fishing from watercraft fly anglers do not crowd other anglers or craft. They do not block entrances to bays or otherwise impede others. Fly anglers do not unnecessarily disturb the water by improperly lowering anchors or slapping the water with paddles or oars.

- Fly anglers always compliment other anglers and promote this Code of Angling Ethics to them whether they fish with a fly or not.

Index

A

Adams, 73, 76, 87, 104
adfluvial trout, 48
alevin, 50
American Fishing Tackle Manufacturers Association (AFTMA), 18
anadromous trout, 6, 9, 48, 49, 58, 112
aquatic insects, general overview, 64
Atlantic salmon flies, 84

B

balanced fly outfit, 18
bass, 12, 18, 20, 61, 101
Bead-headed, Gold-ribbed Hares-ear Nymph, 82
Bend, Oregon, 11
Berners, Dame Juliana, 119
Big Wood River, Idaho, 12
biological diversity, 16
Black Beetle, 78
Blue dun fly pattern, 81
bluegill, 58, 61
boats for lake fishing, 103
bobber, sometimes known as a "strike indicator", 94, 98, 115
Brad's Brat fly pattern, 120, 121
Bradner, Enos, 120, 121
British Columbia, 8, 10, 59, 62, 122
brook trout, 49, 62, 127
brown trout, 7, 11, 47, 50, **57**, 58, 68, 109, 122, 127
bull trout, 62
button-hook mend, 94

C

caddis larvae, 67
caddis pupae, 67
caddisflies, 49, 64, 66, 67, 68, 70, 77, 80, 82, 97, 122
Cascade Mountains, 4, 7, 10, 11, 13, 111
casting, 1, 18, 19, 22, 25, 29, 30, 32, **35**, 36, 37, 39, 41, 42, 43, 45, 58, 73, 89, 91, 94, 105, 108, 123, 124
Century Drive, 11
chironomids, 70
classic dry flies, 76
classic wet flies, 81
Clearwater River, 12
clinch knot, 27, 32
Coastal Mountain Range, 9
coho salmon, 9
Columbia Basin, 10, 11
Columbia River, 4, 10, 11, 12, 15, 49, 111
Cowlitz River, 9, 15
Crab Creek, 10
crappie, 58, 61
Crooked River, 11
cutthroat trout, 7, 9, 16, 47, **56**, 58, 69, 122, 124
    coastal cutthroat, 7, 49, 56

Lahontan cutthroat, 7
sea-run cutthroat, 4, 8, 9, 16, 56, 86, 92, 114, 120, 121
westslope cutthroat, 7

D

damselflies, 7, 70, 71
Deer Creek, tributary to the North Fork Stillaguamish River, 119, 120, 121
Deschutes River, 11, 12, 49, 55, 66, 113
Dolly Varden, 62, 120, 127
double taper fly line, 20
downstream dry fly presentation, 96
down-wing dry flies, 77
drag system of fly reel, 26
dragonflies, 70, 71

E

elitism in fly fishing, 113
Elk-hair Caddis, 6, 77, 87
Elwa River, 16

F

false casting, 42
fiberglass fly rods, 21
fish's life cycle, 49, 63, 67
Fly Fishers International (FFI), 112
fly floatant, 33
fly keeper, 31
fly line, 18, **19**, 20, 21, 23, 24, 26, 27, 30, 31, 35, 41, 42, 43, 46
fly line tapers, 19
fly pattern, definition, 75
fly reel, 98
fly reels, 19, 21, **26**, 27, 29, 30, 31, 32, 33, 35, 46
fly rod, 18, 19, 21, 22, **23**, 32, 33, 35, 36, 54, 61, 102, 109
fly types, definition, 75
fry, 50, 51, 59

G

gape, of hook, 24
gene bank rivers, 16
Greased Line Fishing for Salmon, book by A.H.E. Wood, 92, 93, 125
Grey, Zane, 119

H

Haig-Brown, Roderick, 75, 114, 120, 122
half-pounder steelhead, 13
hatchery trout, 59
Hemingway, Ernest, 12, 123
high-sticking, 95
hooks, 24, 116
hydroelectric power, 15

130

Made in United States
Orlando, FL
31 October 2022

24063199R00076